D0405676

PRAISE FOR *DECLUTTER LIKE A MOTHER*

"If you need powerful and guilt-free encouragement to live simply as a busy mom, you need this book. We all need to cut out some of the clutter in our lives that prevents us from experiencing true freedom and joy. Not only has Allie mastered that, but her passion for seeing you walk in that same freedom is felt in every page of this book."
—JOSHUA BECKER, FOUNDER OF BECOMING MINIMALIST

"Whether you have multiple littles or are just establishing your household, this book is a gift. Allie brilliantly teaches while guiding like a best girlfriend, making simplifying un-intimidating and completely doable. This book is a gift to a world of busy women hustling, striving, and stretching ourselves thin just to keep up and carry a load we were never meant to bear."
—JORDAN LEE DOOLEY, *WALL STREET JOURNAL* BESTSELLING AUTHOR OF *OWN YOUR EVERYDAY*

"Allie understands the influence that clutter can have over our mental health, and the guilt and stress that are often associated with clutter as a working mom or a female professional. In her incredible new book, Allie shows readers how to create space in their lives for the things that matter most—the things that bring them the most joy and help them achieve their best potential. I teach people how to manage their minds, and Allie teaches people how to manage their lives, which is equally important. This book is a must-read for anyone looking to improve their lifestyle and health!"
— DR. CAROLINE LEAF, NEUROSCIENTIST, MENTAL HEALTH AND MIND EXPERT, AND BESTSELLING AUTHOR OF *SWITCH ON YOUR BRAIN* AND *CLEANING UP YOUR MENTAL MESS*

"At almost every line in the book, I shook my head saying 'amen.' I felt Allie's words deeply because I was her. I am her still, and I need saving from my stuff! I love Allie's actionable tips and her funny and real writing style. This book is going to help so many people—myself included. Now, BRB [be right back], I'm going to purge my bathroom cabinets!"
—SUZY HOLMAN, FOUNDER OF SUZY SCHOOL

"Do you want to live a more fulfilling life and give energy and passion to the things that really matter? Then *Declutter Like a Mother* is your book! It's a game changer for your home and your family. Allie's radical authenticity is contagious and will absolutely inspire you to show up as YOU. Allie's work has been infinitely helpful to me and has shown me what matters most. My hope is that the same holds true for you."

—ANGIE LEE, HOST OF *THE ANGIE LEE SHOW* PODCAST

"Allie Casazza has written a book every mom needs to read. If you have ever felt not good enough or that your day is spent chasing perfection, *Declutter Like a Mother* is the book you have been waiting for. It's an invitation to trade the clutter and noise in your life with wholeness and grace. It's a wake-up call and a strong reminder to stop filling your days (and your home) with 'things' and instead choose to dig deep into the mother you long to be."

— TANYA DALTON, BESTSELLING AUTHOR OF *THE JOY OF MISSING OUT* AND FOUNDER OF THE INTENTIONAL CEO

"Allie is the real deal. She is honest and encouraging, and she gives practical help that every woman can use to declutter her home and life. If you need a new best friend who will give you the light-hearted kick in the pants, *Declutter Like a Mother* is the perfect book for you!"

—ALLI WORTHINGTON, BESTSELLING AUTHOR, BUSINESS COACH, AND ENTREPRENEUR

"Do yourself a favor and soak up every single word in the pages of this book! This is life giving, not just for moms but for everyone. Allie shares her personal journey while giving you the tools you need to declutter every area of your life. What I love most about this book is that it isn't about stuff, but about how stuff affects our mental health. I love how real Allie is. She is refreshing and needed in today's world."

—CATHY HELLER, HOST OF *DON'T KEEP YOUR DAY JOB* PODCAST

"Warning: After reading this book, your life will get a major upgrade! My inner and outer world made a quantum leap the moment Allie came into my life. Her delightfully witty, compassionate, and endearing vibe is a breath of fresh air to all moms (new and seasoned) who are searching for ease, reassurance, and a clear path to a lighter, less cluttered, and more meaningful life. This book is a shining light for those of us who are craving a mom friend in our lives who 'gets it' and will hype us up and keep it real. *Declutter Like a Mother* is a life changer, and I can't think of anyone more perfect to pen it than the incomparable Allie Casazza."

—JILL STANTON, FOUNDER OF MILLIONAIRE GIRLS CLUB AND COFOUNDER OF SCREW THE NINE TO FIVE

"Allie is the friend and coach that every woman/mother needs! Her ability to break down the overwhelming act of clearing out clutter into realistic and practical steps is second to none. Allie walks you through the decluttering process every step of the way, and unlike most books that keep it surface level and purely focused on baskets and bins, Allie addresses meaningful issues that are bound to come up, such as relationships, emotions, boundaries, maintenance mode, and so much more. *Declutter Like a Mother* will make your life lighter and your mood brighter, so that you can show up in your life as the best version of yourself. I can't recommend this book enough!"

—ROBIN LONG, FOUNDER AND CEO OF THE BALANCED LIFE

"I feel seen, and my feelings feel validated. Allie's storytelling gives permission to feel overwhelmed, not only to the modern mother but also to the generations to follow. Decluttering is way beyond 'stuff,' and this book is an essential read for those who want to feel lighter."

—HEATHER CHAUVIN, AUTHOR OF *DYING TO BE A GOOD MOTHER*

DECLUTTER

LIKE A

MOTHER

DECLUTTER
LIKE A
MOTHER

A GUILT-FREE, NO-STRESS WAY TO
TRANSFORM YOUR HOME AND YOUR LIFE

ALLIE CASAZZA

NELSON
BOOKS

An Imprint of Thomas Nelson

Declutter Like a Mother

© 2021 Allie Casazza

All rights reserved. No portion of this book may be reproduced, stored in a retrieval system, or transmitted in any form or by any means—electronic, mechanical, photocopy, recording, scanning, or other—except for brief quotations in critical reviews or articles, without the prior written permission of the publisher.

Published in Nashville, Tennessee, by Nelson Books, an imprint of Thomas Nelson. Nelson Books and Thomas Nelson are registered trademarks of HarperCollins Christian Publishing, Inc.

Published in association with literary agent Jenni Burke of Illuminate Literary Agency, www.illuminateliterary.com.

Thomas Nelson titles may be purchased in bulk for educational, business, fundraising, or sales promotional use. For information, please e-mail SpecialMarkets@ThomasNelson.com.

Scripture quotations are taken from the Revised Standard Version of the Bible. Copyright © 1946, 1952, and 1971 National Council of the Churches of Christ in the United States of America. Used by permission. All rights reserved worldwide.

Any internet addresses, phone numbers, or company or product information printed in this book are offered as a resource and are not intended in any way to be or to imply an endorsement by Thomas Nelson, nor does Thomas Nelson vouch for the existence, content, or services of these sites, phone numbers, companies, or products beyond the life of this book.

Library of Congress Cataloging-in-Publication Data

Names: Casazza, Allie, 1987-author.
Title: Declutter like a mother: a guilt-free, no-stress way to transform your home and your life / Allie Casazza.
Description: Nashville, Tennessee: Nelson Books, an imprint of Thomas Nelson, [2021] | Includes bibliographical references. | Summary: "Successful business entrepreneur Allie Casazza shares her powerful and proven method for clearing the clutter in our minds by first clearing the clutter in our homes, the place where transformation begins"—Provided by publisher.
Identifiers: LCCN 2020053640 (print) | LCCN 2020053641 (ebook) | ISBN 9781400225637 (HC) | ISBN 9781400225644 (ePub) | ISBN 9781400225651 (Audio)
Subjects: LCSH: Storage in the home. | House cleaning.
Classification: LCC TX324.5 .C37 2021 (print) | LCC TX324.5 (ebook) | DDC 648/.8—dc23
LC record available at https://lccn.loc.gov/2020053640
LC ebook record available at https://lccn.loc.gov/2020053641

Printed in the United States of America

21 22 23 24 25 LSC 10 9 8 7 6 5 4 3 2 1

This book is dedicated to my younger self.

That exhausted, struggling version of me who was trying so damn hard to make it all happen and be a good mom without realizing things could be simpler, without realizing she was already good, just as she was.

She is not just me; she is also my mom, who has told me so many times that she wishes she'd had a message like this when she was raising kids.

She is every woman who is stuck, overwhelmed, and wants more time for what matters.

That version of me was trying so hard, exhausting herself every day without signs of progress. She deserves the credit for this book and its message. She was stronger than she realized. She was doing the very best she could. She needs to know that.

And so do you.

CONTENTS

CONTENTS

INTRODUCTION

I FELT DEFEATED. AGAIN.

I sat there on my couch, next to a gigantic pile of laundry, and it was clear which of us was winning. Another day had come and gone, and I had barely been able to keep up. Was I the only mom in the world who felt like she just couldn't hold it all together? The days were flying by me. I had three kids under three years old, and even though my oldest was still so little, I felt like I was already missing so much of my kids' childhoods. I was always busy cleaning up the stuff; always running around reacting to problems.

At night when I dropped into bed exhausted, my day would flash before me, and all I saw were piles of dishes, the endless mountain of laundry, toys and books and markers and jackets and shoes and empty water bottles and paper artwork that all needed to be picked up. So much stuff.

I thought I was supposed to enjoy the time raising my kids, but I realized I wasn't spending enough quality time with them to enjoy it. I felt like I had to keep moving or the house and the day would collapse into total chaos. When I did press pause to spend time with them, it felt like I had to pay the price later—catching up on housework and making up for the time I missed cleaning in order to live my life.

It's not that I'm a neat freak, and I wasn't a hoarder, either. All this work was simply to keep the house functioning. It seemed that in motherhood, I was like the student in school who stays up all night studying and still gets a C– on the exam.

I felt like I was carrying around a dark secret I couldn't tell anyone. The secret was, I woke up every morning already too exhausted to take on a day that hadn't even started yet. I felt completely depleted, depressed, miserable all the time. And for that, **I felt so guilty.**

For so long I carried this secret around, pretending to be okay at mommy meetups, at the park, at get-togethers with friends who seemed to be doing great, at church—everywhere I went, I held up a mask to hide my secret. I needed to let it out. I needed to talk to someone. I needed to see if anyone else felt this way in motherhood.

Maybe it was normal. Maybe everyone was pretending. Maybe there was an answer I wasn't aware of to make everything better.

I mentioned being overwhelmed and my unhappiness to several women I respected who were way ahead of me in the journey of motherhood. Although phrased differently, of course, their responses were all the same.

"Yup, that's motherhood! It's crazy. And just wait 'til they get older! It gets even harder in different ways! But don't worry, you'll get through it."

The hopelessness I felt hearing this was deafening.

So, this is it?

This is the way it's supposed to be?

And it gets . . . worse?

I felt so heavy.

It seemed like all the mothers of the world had decided it's a total crap show all the time and there's no way out of it. They'd say, "That's just motherhood." They offered no help or hack—it was simply **struggling and draining yourself empty but also carpe-ing all the diems because "it goes by so fast!"**

I thought about a verse I had always clung to since my childhood growing up in the church: "The thief comes only to steal and kill and destroy; I came that they may have life, and have it abundantly" (John 10:10).

Abundant life. If God is good, and God desires for us to experience a life of abundance, of goodness and enjoyment, was this version of life, of motherhood, it?

Not a chance. There's just no way. And maybe that was why it wasn't sitting right with me.

So, what then? What was the answer? What shifts needed to happen for me to step into that kind of abundant life and out of this one?

One day while I was processing the "advice" from the women I'd talked with, I was having a particularly hard time with the kids. There were meltdowns and diaper explosions and so many messes and spills. I was about to snap. I could feel it welling up in me.

I quickly turned on the TV for the kids, set the baby in his bouncer, and ran up the stairs to be alone. I was already sobbing as I slammed the door to my bathroom and slid down the wall, falling into a heap on the floor in absolute hopelessness.

God! Where are you? What do I do here? I want out! I don't want to be a mom anymore. Not this way. Help me. Please wake up and help me.

I kind of hate saying that I had an epiphany, because I feel like everyone says that. But that's what it was. It was like I came out of my body and could see myself, my life, my kids, how I was spending my days—all from an aerial perspective. And it was heartbreaking.

And then a thought popped into my head: *What exactly are you spending all your time doing?*

Picking up. Maintaining my life. Maintaining . . . stuff. Stuff we don't even need.

Boom. That was it.

There was so. much. stuff. everywhere.

I suddenly knew exactly what to do. It was a little crazy, and I wasn't sure if it would work, but I was desperate, and it was worth a shot. I made dinner, got the kids in bed early, and went into their playroom—the room that had become the bane of my existence.

The room was full of colorful bins, each one overflowing with jumbled toys. There were toys scattered across the floor, in chests, in boxes—everywhere. I would send my kids in here to play and they would regularly come out less than five minutes later complaining of boredom. This room was pointless, and I'd had enough.

I began working through the room, making piles: **keep, trash, donate.** I got rid of every single toy that I felt wasn't benefiting my kids. If I was going to have to clean something up, it was going to be things that added value to our lives— things my family needed and loved.

When I finished decluttering that room, all that remained were toys I'd seen my kids use to engage in constructive or imaginary play: trains and tracks, a couple of dress-up costumes, books, and blocks. The trunk of my car was overstuffed with toys to donate, and our playroom felt clear and spacious. I immediately felt lighter.

The next morning after breakfast, I sat on the couch with the baby and sent my two- and three-year-olds into their playroom, curious to see if meltdowns would ensue because of what I'd done. They walked in and I heard my three-year-old yell, "Hey! It's clean in here!" and they happily started playing.

I was shocked. I relaxed into the sofa and enjoyed my first hot cup of coffee in two years.

To my surprise, the kids played in that room for three hours that day. *Three hours!* Just in case you're not aware, three hours of uninterrupted play for two toddlers is insane—especially when their previous record was two seconds. It wasn't just that day either. They continued to want to be in their playroom for long periods of time from then on.

I didn't know it at the time, but kids actually thrive when they're not overwhelmed with options. My kids were overstimulated by the massive amount of toys in their playroom, and it was causing a general feeling of anxiety for me and for them. Our house was fostering an environment of tension. Once the room was decluttered and organized, they played and interacted with each other more and for longer periods of time. They created scenarios and stories and played make believe.

Fewer options inside created the opportunity for more outside play. I had always wanted my kids to spend time outdoors and know what it's like to make mud pies, find ant hills, collect leaves and sticks and rocks, and have picnic lunches in the grass. On one particular day, I was sitting in the California sunshine watching them play and thinking: *Why haven't we done this more?*

It was as if I had freed their God-given gift of imagination and given them the joy of childhood when I cleared out the mountain of toys.

After observing what decluttering had done for my kids, I started purging other areas of the house—the bathroom, the kitchen, the closets and cupboards—and our entire home began to transform. Now that I was spending less than half the time managing my house, I was actually able to have fun playing with my kids. I also found the courage to take up homeschooling. (*What?* I never thought that could happen!) My marriage improved because I was a happier version of myself. My depression lifted, and I felt like my days were much more aligned with the kind of life I wanted to live.

Our stuff wasn't waging war on me anymore, because I had removed the unnecessary things. It was all out of my way. Life felt lighter, intentional, and I was no longer simply "getting through it." This was abundant life rising up. I could feel it.

Today, years later, we've had a fourth baby, traveled a ton, and I run a business doing what I love: helping other women simplify their lives, from home to schedule to business. Housework is just a sidenote in my life. It's something I maintain a little each day to serve my family and keep things running smoothly; it does not take up the bulk of my life.

My kids' imaginations continue to bloom in amazing ways without the overstimulation of too many toys, and they get along so much better than they used to. I feel like we're giving them a meaningful childhood, and I love that.

So why did decluttering provide so much freedom? What did excess stuff have to do with my depression and general lack of joy?

Our homes are overflowing with stuff and we're drowning with no lifeline in sight. We keep thinking our possessions will make us happy, so we keep collecting more. But they're not making us happy; they're weighing us down, pulling us under. Our overabundance is affecting us negatively. And not just us, but our families too. Our physical health, our mental health, our relationships are all suffering because we have *too much stuff.*

Modern research studies show a direct link between the amount of physical possessions in a house and the stress level of the female homeowner. One study done at UCLA found that the more stuff there was in a woman's house, the higher her level of stress hormones. This same study also found that women subconsciously relate how happy they are with their families and home lives to how they feel about their homes. So, the more clutter and chaos in her home, the less happy a woman is with her family and her life.[1]

Bingo.

That's what was going on with me, and I believe it's the cause of today's epidemic of burnout in motherhood.

By the time I made this connection, I had been blogging for a couple of years as a hobby. As a stay-at-home mom, blogging was an outlet for me. Writing about what I was figuring out in motherhood was a way to release stress. As I made these changes in my life, I began sharing them on my blog.

I decided to create a business from my blog so I could teach other women how to make these life changes in simple, doable, effective ways. I shared my story about removing clutter in an article called "How Getting Rid of My Stuff Saved My Motherhood."[2] To my surprise, it went viral. There were even a few days when my story was trending above the first presidential debate of 2016!

I've now reached millions with this message, which reveals how much it's needed. If I was the only one experiencing chronic overwhelm, my story wouldn't have gone viral. I wouldn't have thousands of women enrolling in my programs and sharing their transformations with me every day.

I've traveled the country to help women clear their clutter. I've supported a widow as she sorted through her late husband's closet. I've guided a mom struggling with depression as she cleared out the kids' overstuffed playroom. I've helped a hoarder go through her garage. I've stood next to a woman in her closet while she grappled with the realization that she hated her body as she looked at all the clothes she owned but never wore. I've seen a lot.

What I've realized in my years of doing this work is that our stuff is connected to emotions about decisions we have not yet made and truths we are avoiding. I've also realized that most mothers are barely getting by, living in survival mode, feeling like their kids' childhoods are passing them by even as they're growing up right there in front of them. I have observed that clutter leads to a feeling of chronic over-whelm, and that is the root of the "Hot Mess Mom" culture almost everyone subscribes to. What I do for women is the opposite of this. It's freedom; it's creating space to actually be present in your life for your kids. This is my passion.

Our stuff is literally stealing from us. It's stealing the most precious thing in the world: life. Marshall Goldsmith wrote in his book *Triggers*, "If we do not create and control our environment, our environment creates and controls us."[3] We need to take control back. We need to set our homes up to reflect our values, so our homes are not constantly pulling us away from what's most important.

That's what moms need more than anything else. The type of minimalism that means less cleaning, less stress, less distraction from the people they most care about—and more energy and free time to focus on their priorities. They want to feel the joy of always being ready for company to drop by without stress, worry, or embarrassment. They want to enjoy their home rather than be owned by it. They want to be the mom who plays rather than the mom who's always cleaning up. They want to be a happier person.

This is about making space for you to do good work—the work you're called to do, whether that's the work of being a stay-at-home mom or the CEO of a company, or both. Whatever your lifestyle is, I want to help you create space to live it well.

If you're ready to make some of the same changes I made that led me to this place of thriving in life and opting out of mere survival mode, you're in the right place, friend. I want this for you. I want you to know it doesn't have to be like this for one more day. You can choose a different path, you can thrive, you can love and enjoy this life, you can escape the chronic overwhelm that everyone else calls normal.

I know you want to be the best mom you can possibly be. I know you want to show up for this life, for your kids' childhoods. I know you want more than the status quo.

Decluttering like a mother changed my life, and it will work for you too. I promise you, it's so worth it. You have the power to change your story.

A NOTE BEFORE WE START

This book is written from my experience as a privileged, white, Cuban American woman. Because this has been my experience, I can't claim to know other experiences. Everyone, regardless of background or circumstance, is welcome here. If there is something for you in this book, please take it.

My intention for this book is to change the lives of women everywhere and to lighten the load you may be carrying by changing the way your home feels.

I will show you how minimalism can fit into your life, specifically into whatever area of your house feels heavy. I will make it lighter, easier, so that things work with you and for you. And we're going to do this together.

Let's get started. You've got this. I've got you. We're doing this. Cheers to change, babe!

xo Allie

ONE

THINGS ARE ABOUT TO GET SO. MUCH. LIGHTER.

MINIMALISM IS NOT THE POINT OF THIS BOOK.

Did you just stop reading and flip to the front cover to make sure you picked up the right book? Don't worry if you did. But since we're going to deal with a lot over the course of this journey, I want to make sure we're on the same page before we dive in.

I don't care about the rules. I don't care how other people define minimalism. I really don't even care about minimalism itself. For me, it's simply a means to get to the goal of a better, lighter life. I'm definitely not interested in the one-size-fits-all approach to minimalism that has taken the world by storm the past few years. You know the kind I'm talking about. It's the kind that only works if you're single or bored or don't have kids.

I don't care if you call what I do minimalism. I'm using

that word because that's what everyone else calls the removal of excess stuff. I needed a well-known word to express what it was that took me from feeling overwhelmed, depressed, overcomplicated, and over-burdened to feeling light, joyful, present, and purposeful in my life. But maybe the word I'm looking for is *less*. Maybe it's *simplicity*. Maybe it's *intentionality*. Or maybe I need to make up my own word. How about *simplicitism*? That feels a bit better, but it's a mouthful. And it's not really a word, but it's fine.

Whatever we call it, it's about being intentional. It's about simplifying. **It's about having less of what doesn't matter in order to make room for what does.**

Generally, I think most people would envision minimalism as empty white rooms with a few succulents on the counter, like Kim Kardashian's bathroom.

If you picked up this book, chances are you're a mom (though you might be a dad or a grandmother or just a person who likes the cover of this book). And if you're someone even remotely like me, then the white-on-white-barely-furnished-perfectly-clean-rooms kind of minimalism isn't going to work for you. I mean, come on. I'm a working mom of four kids (and counting) who are home-educated, and I run an active business with my husband from our home. If I tried to subscribe to the kind of minimalism that a lot of other people subscribe to, I would fail. Epically.

It's not that I am a failure at minimalism; it's just that that type of minimalism doesn't work for my life. If it's not relative to me and my family, what's the point? Pursuing that type of minimalism for the sake of wide-open, empty space doesn't fit into a life full of noisy, playful kids and all the messes that come from having a good time.

So, what kind of minimalism do moms need? *Moms need the kind of minimalism that works for them.*

Take a second to let the simplicity of that sink in. The kind of minimalism moms need is the kind that works for moms. It's the kind that helps you, the kind that supports you, the kind that makes you feel lighter without making you feel like there's a massive set of unrealistic rules you need to follow. It's the kind of minimalism that is relative to the family you're raising, the home you live in, the climate in your region, whether you live in a suburb or a city, and most importantly, the story you're telling with your life and home.

Your home is a reflection of your life's story. If the minimalism you're implementing isn't relative to the story you're telling, you're going to end up getting rid of stuff just for the sake of having less. This kind of rigid, rules-based minimalism can end up being the opposite of freeing. It can leave you obsessing over the number of things you have in your home rather than creating space for life to happen and actually resting in the enjoyment of it.

That being said, you obviously don't need to keep every single thing in your house. That also wouldn't support you in being present for your life. Minimalism that works is all about balance. Most of the time, things are just things, but we overcomplicate them by attaching meaning to objects. Here's the foundation I need you to understand: **what takes up your space takes up your time.**

Let's use a basic household appliance to demonstrate my

point. I'm going to go with the toaster. Whether you have a toaster or a toaster oven, it's safe to assume you probably have some sort of bread-crisping apparatus in your home. Don't get hung up on the appliance, insert whatever you have in your kitchen and just work with me.

Your toaster sits on your kitchen counter waiting to be used. It doesn't seem like it requires very much of you, and it doesn't even take up that much space. But because it's there, you use it. It requires you to empty out the crumb tray, wipe it down, and clean around it or pick it up to clean underneath it (on the days you care enough to do so). Even something as inconspicuous as a toaster that just sits there takes up your time every so often.

Let's estimate that it takes about two seconds to put the bread in the toaster and push the handle down, and then two more seconds to turn it off and get the bread out. Let's say that it takes about ten seconds to dump out the crumb tray and wipe it down, and then ten more seconds to clean the front of the toaster. Let's add ten more seconds for a once-per-week, deep-cleaning day where you wipe the counter under the toaster and make it shiny. That's approximately 178 seconds a week.

That's 9,256 seconds a year.

That's over 154 minutes a year.

That's over 2.5 hours a year spent *on your freakin' toaster*.

Now, think about every single thing in your house. Think about every sock, every shoe, every photograph, every piece of decor, every notepad, every bobby pin, every piece of paper, every board game, every cord, every toy . . . every single thing taking up some amount of your time.

This. Adds. Up.

Do you see my point? Every single thing that takes up space in your home is also taking up some amount of your time. Let this be a reminder that you're not a failure at this. You're overwhelmed because this is *a lot*.

If we want change, we need to face the things that are holding us back. We often overcomplicate our lives by overstuffing our homes and making our lives harder than they need to be. We give our time to things that don't ultimately matter, and then complain that there isn't enough time in the day.

So what do I get rid of, Allie? you might be asking. *How can I fix this? My brain hurts even thinking about it.*

Don't worry. I got you. That question is the very reason I wrote this book. I know that decision making is often the most tiring thing in the world. Decision fatigue is a real thing.[4] As moms, decision making is literally what we do all day. We make decisions for everyone. How many times during your sixteen-plus waking hours do you hear these questions?

Can I have cereal?
Can I have a snack?
Can I watch *Mulan*?
Can I have a popsicle?
Can I jump on the trampoline?
Do I have to take a nap?
Can I go outside?
Can we have a dog?
Can we get rid of my brother?
What's for dinner?

Mom?

Mom?

Mom?

It's constant. And it's exhausting. The absolute last thing you need in your daily life is more decisions you need to make. That's where I come in.

Listen. Getting clutter out of your way is something that will help you. Since you've chosen to read this book, it's likely there is some sort of heaviness in your home, a sense of too much, and it's having a major effect on your life. You want to improve the way you talk, the way you interact with your kids, the way your day unfolds. Maybe you're so deep down the rabbit hole that what you're feeling seems a lot like despair. Or maybe things are going okay, and you simply like self-improvement and want to make things even better. Whatever your situation and your reasons, minimalism is whatever you need it to be as long as you're asking this question: **Is this aligning with the life I want to live?**

I want to help you answer that question and make decisions in the areas of your home that feel heavy. I'm going to add a little bit of decision making to your plate now, but it will result in fewer day-to-day decisions when all is said and done. I want to come alongside you and help you get rid of the unnecessary bulk, the heaviness, the excess that doesn't need to be there. And I want to do it in a way that feels relative to you and the family you're raising.

What I want is for you to make a version of minimalism (or simplicitism or whatever you need to call it) that is unique to you and your family. I want to give you the gift of *less of what doesn't matter* for the sake of *more of what does matter*. Start by asking yourself: Is my house working for me or against me? If you feel as though your house is working against you, it is not supporting you, which is the opposite of what it is meant to do.

I'm going to show you how minimalism can address the areas of your home that feel heavy and make them work with you and for you. To give you some motivation and inspiration, use your imagination to jump forward in time and take a look at what your life will look like in the very near future after you have practiced what's in this book.

If you start to feel overwhelmed while trying to climb out of the overwhelm, I want you to picture what you're working toward. If you get stuck in the details and sorting through a room of your house feels like too much, like you're stuck in the muck with no end in sight, I want you to know that there *is* an end, and it is not far away.

So let's jump into the future and imagine a few scenarios.

SCENARIO 1: You come home at the end of a long day with your arms full of groceries. You open the door and immediately feel at peace. Your home is restful. It's nice. It's welcoming. It's just what you need after a long day of getting stuff done. You're not wading through a mess and envisioning an endless list of chores in your head. Nope! Your task list is checked off for the day. It's time to put the groceries away in a kitchen you feel good in, make dinner, relax, and enjoy your family.

SCENARIO 2: Dinner is finished, the kids had their baths and are in bed, and it's time for you to start your end-of-the-day routine. Instead of running around the house overwhelmed by the mess left over from the day and trying to clean every single surface so you can have some semblance of peace before you crash into bed, you calmly walk through your house, picking up a few things here and there. You wipe down the kitchen counters, put a small load of folded laundry in the dresser, toss a pair of dirty socks in the hamper. It takes you twenty minutes, and then you're able to sit down with a glass of wine or a cup of tea and breathe. You can relax because everything is done, and it didn't take hours.

SCENARIO 3: You wake up in the morning, open your eyes, and the first thing you see is a neat room. A relaxing haven. You get ready in a bathroom that's functional and tidy. You walk downstairs and make breakfast in a clean and organized kitchen. Your day automatically starts with good energy, not stress. Your phone alerts you to a text message from your mother-in-law saying she's going to drop by real quick to bring you something. Instead of feeling panicked and shoveling things behind the shower curtain (that was always my go-to hiding spot), you're ready. Your house is lived-in and normal. Sure, there are shoes by the front door, cords coming out from the TV cabinet, and a few scattered things here and there (because, hey, people live here), but it's not a mess. There is nothing for you to freak out about. Your home is easy to run. Everything has a place. You're not constantly cleaning because the clutter is gone and it's not possible for your home to get *that* chaotic. Less than an hour a day is all you need to keep your home clean.

———

Some of you might be like, "Girl, this is a load of bulllll."

I know this may be *so far* from your reality. I get it. But I don't want you to buy into the belief that none of this is possible. That's not true. No matter how far from your current reality these scenarios are—and the exact details may not apply to you because your life is different—the peace; the lack of added, unnecessary stress; and the part about your home being a haven that supports you is possible for every single person reading this.

Several years ago, my family and I moved from Southern California to the Midwest. I had absolutely no family and no friends anywhere nearby, and I was so, so lonely. I was working on making new friends and had plans with another mom I'd met to spend the afternoon at the park with our kids, but it started pouring rain before we could even leave our houses.

My phone dinged with a text from her: "I don't think we can go to the park today and my house is being painted. Can we come to you?"

Let me tell you, if I'd received that text a couple of years earlier, I would have been standing in a monsoon made of my own tears and snot. Panic would have shot through my body, and I would have hidden in the hallway closet simultaneously crying and yelling, "I just want to make friends! Why, God, *why*?" (Because, at one time, I was a stable adult like that.)

But you know what? I didn't feel or say any of those things that day. Instead, I was able to text back, "Sure, come on over!" I didn't have to run around, yelling at the kids to help while doing the shove-everything-under-the-couches thing. My house wasn't perfect, but it was fine; she could come over as it was, and that's all that mattered to me. Perfectly staged to impress was not my goal when I cleared the clutter a few years earlier. I just wanted to remove the cause of excess stress and be able to have days like this when I could welcome a friend over without the panic. I had reclaimed the freedom that clutter had once stolen from me.

Friend, please hear me when I say, this process we're going through is not about trying to create a home where things are perfect; it's about creating a home where things are so much *lighter*. It's about creating a world in which we are available for life—the good parts and the hard parts—and aren't making things even harder on ourselves. A world where we don't feel stress and negative energy all day every day but instead have more clarity and more space.

Over the years, I've talked to a lot of women, from coaching calls to in-person meetings to interacting during my live streams, and one thing has stayed consistently true with every story I hear: **changing your home is a means to an end.** It's a strategy we can use to create more space for living. It's the catalyst to a life that excites you and feels good. It's step one to less stress.

Decluttering won't make everything perfect and it won't solve all your problems, but it will make things so much lighter.

Purging my home created less need for me to spend my physical and mental energy on things that didn't matter to me. Yes, I still struggled with some of the same old things. I still ate junk food and chose the chalupa over the salad more times than was healthy. I still snapped at my kids when I was really frustrated. I still had emotional outbursts. I was still a human being. But the negativity in my day decreased significantly, and I was no longer making things even harder on myself by creating more work.

I found that I had more patience. I was more fun to be around. I woke up excited for the day instead of dreading it. That's a huge win when you're a mom of three under three, which is what I was at the time.

Fast-forward to today and my life is so different. So much lighter and freer than it would have been if I had stayed on the path I was on before simplicity changed my trajectory. I now have four kids and homeschool them while my husband and I run a successful business. There's a lot of people in our home, and we are home all the time. There's no way I would have been able to handle all of this before minimalism entered my life.

Let me be real. My life felt like a total shit show. I was the "Hot Mess Mom" all the time. I barely had time to shower. There was no way I could have fit in starting my own business, let alone growing that business into what it is today, homeschooling my kids, working on my own self-growth, and nurturing my marriage and other relationships. Not a chance.

Removing the excess stuff from my home and learning to live without it ended up being the jumping-off point for so many purposeful things I've ended up doing in my life. I was able to say yes to many amazing opportunities and experiences, resulting in personal growth and family fun. I was able to implement the business ideas I had flowing out of me, because my home wasn't stealing time and energy anymore; it was actually supporting me.

And girl, that's the whole point. That's why I don't want you to get bogged down in the details. That's why I don't want you to obsess over counting your items. I just want you to walk into your home, trash bags in hand, and *decide* that you're done with the old way of doing things and ready to bring in change.

I want you to feel that fire, feel that energy rising up in you. I want you to feel that fighter in you coming to life, because this is so important. You're fighting for your life here. You're fighting for space, for peace, for time. This isn't about spending every ounce of the time and energy you have making sure everything is as minimal as humanly possible. I don't want that for you. I do want your life to be lighter and more focused on what really matters to you. That's what I want you to fight for.

Too often, moms play the victim to their lives. We play victim to our kids, to our homes, to our circumstances, when, really, we're the ones in charge. **We just need to take ownership of what is ours.**

I can help you move from victim to victor, friend. I have the solution. It won't be perfect. It won't solve every problem you have. But we're not shooting for perfection, remember? We're shooting for less stress, more space; less chaos, more peace; less of what doesn't matter, more of what does.

I believe we are called to live an abundant life. From the way motherhood is talked about, society acts like moms are excluded from that life. But I know we're not. I know moms can live abundantly as much as everybody else. So that's what we're shooting for. That's what we're going to take a hold of: living more abundantly; living from a place of ownership, not victimhood.

Listen, there are going to be problems and stresses and family issues, because we're real people living real lives. You'll have messy days, but the resistance will be gone. It's a lot easier to walk through life and its different seasons when you're not pressured, stressed out, and heavily burdened.

You are not meant for a life of survival mode, mama. You are meant for abundance! You have within you the ability to create this, and it all starts with clearing physical space for what matters most to you.

Since you're not there yet, I'm going to give you some prompts to help you envision the changes you could make to start living this way. Keep your eye on the results, not the process!

- How would you feel if there was less laundry to do? Imagine everyone in your home having the clothes they need, they like, and they can actually wear. There wouldn't be a crazy amount of excess clothes ending up in the hampers or on the floor, so you'd be able to stay on top of it, and Laundry Mountain would be a thing of the past.
- How would you feel if cleaning the kitchen after dinner each night didn't take you over an hour? What if you could finish dinner, clean up, put the kids to bed, and

still have time to relax and enjoy your night? Or maybe still have the energy to work on that passion project you've been putting off?

- How would you feel if your house was a space where your kids could freely play, create, and grow because it wasn't overrun by clutter? How would you feel to have less of their stuff take over the house?
- How would you feel if you had way less housework every day?
- How would you feel if your relationships changed for the better because you were less stressed out on a daily basis? How would you feel if your marriage and your friendships and the way you mother your kids improved?

Don't you feel like if these things were to actually happen, your life would be so much better? Of course you do! Even if it's hard to imagine a world in which you're not stepping on a LEGO every time you round a corner (let me be clear—sometimes I still step on a LEGO in my house, and yes, I curse hard and loud), this less stressful, more intentional home *can* happen for you. This is what your life will look like in just a few weeks' time if you're willing to do the work and implement the simple strategies in this book. It is absolutely possible.

You are in charge of your life. You don't have to play the victim one second longer. I'm not saying things haven't been hard for you. I'm not belittling any of the experiences that led you here. But from this point forward, you get to make the decision for how you want your life to go. You get to set yourself—and your home—free.

Are you ready for me to show you how? It's time to get up and do this. I think you finally understand what's at stake. I think you get what's waiting for you at the end of the tunnel. The time to start is now!

TIP: You're going to want to take a before photo! I know it's painful and you would rather not capture the mess. But trust me, *everyone* regrets not snapping one before they start. Make sure you take photos of your progress. I would love to connect with you on this journey. It's my favorite thing. Tag me in your before and after photos on Instagram @allie_thatsme.

EVERYTHING YOU NEED TO KNOW ABOUT CLUTTER (SO YOU CAN GET IT *ALL OUT*)

HERE'S WHAT YOU NEED TO KNOW BEFORE WE START: this book is based on my annual Declutter Like a Mother® (DLAM) challenge. In this challenge, our mantra is *progress not perfection*. Because here's the thing, there are already so many different voices telling you how to do all the nitty-gritty details of every single thing in your house and exactly how you should have everything set up. But if those well-intentioned opinions have not been serving you, it's time to let me help.

My approach is to help you create real, lasting progress the simplest way possible. Progress that is actually going to put a dent in the chaos and stress you have been handling for far too long. And girl, that is not going to happen by hyper-focusing on how your closet is organized or what the inside of your refrigerator looks like, but rather by working through mental blocks and shifting your thinking about the way your home and life should work, and then using those mental shifts to physically remove the junk without crazy amounts of fear. We're going to go through the main areas of your home and radically purge them, so you *feel* the progress and *see* the results in your family and home.

I want to teach you, as Nate Berkus says, how to be the "ruthless editor" of your space.[5] I'm bringing the DLAM challenge vibes and the expertise from my signature program, Your Uncluttered Home®, into this book the best I can. I've seen tens of thousands of moms transform their lives using my programs (and you'll hear from some of them in this book), so if you want to take that deeper dive, you're invited to enroll anytime.

Many people tend to take more action and retain information a bit better when completing interactive digital courses, so I'm giving a substantial discount on this program that you can use whenever you're ready. (You can sign up for the Your Uncluttered Home program through my website alliecasazza .com/course.) Sometimes, you just need accountability, a community, and more support to make real changes that last.

Lots of people just need help getting started in the main spaces where they can experience results. That's what this book is for. It'll help you to get your head above water. It'll calm your outer chaos, and in doing so your *inner* chaos will lessen too. It is going to give you a massive push—the head start you've been needing.

I'm going to offer some of my best tips and strategies by categorizing them into different focus areas. I'm putting them all in one place for you, so you don't have to keep scouring bookstores and the internet looking for something—anything—that will help you get your shit together. You've been there, done that.

My job is to take the brain work out of it for you. I believe we get in our own way a lot of the time, and my goal is to help you get your overanalyzing brain out of the way and simplify the process of decluttering. **You shouldn't have to spend so much mental energy on your space!**

"I'm just a naturally messy person . . ."

Let me add here: this whole process has nothing to do with whether you are a naturally neat or messy person. This is not about being tidy or "getting organized." This is about taking your *space* back. It's about taking your *time* back. It's about getting the unnecessary crap out of the way and unclogging your mind.

This is a method that will clear that stuck, stagnant energy in your home that comes from having too much stuff. Being neat or messy has nothing to do with it. You can be a naturally messy person (that's me!) and have an uncluttered space. Clutter does not equal messy. Clutter equals clutter, and it's hurting you regardless of whether you're messy or tidy by nature.

HOW IT WORKS

Let me just say, this works. It works no matter how much or how little space you have in your home. It works whether you have no kids or twelve kids. I've seen people in all situations and from all walks of life make these changes and get massive results. I've personally lived out this method with four kids, a cat, and a dog in a twenty-six-foot camper. (Yes, we did this. Yes, we are insane. But it was really fun and we saw a whole lot of our country.) I've lived this out in a janky little house we could barely afford, in a modest medium-sized house, and in a large, expansive house. Simplicity makes life better no matter where or how you live. Minimalism is a tool that can help you focus on what matters whether you live in a mansion or a hut.

In the Declutter Like a Mother online challenge, we focus on a few areas of your home for thirty minutes every day for two weeks. In this book, I've expanded the challenge to cover more than just a few areas. We will talk about the many ways to make it work for your life and schedule, but the most important thing I want you to take away is *focus*. By focus, I don't mean, "I'm gutting this entire room now!" Instead, I mean committing to creating a system that gets you going. Would setting aside an hour a week be helpful for you? Do that. Would setting a timer for thirty minutes once a day help? Do that. If there's a different time or structure that would work better for your life, then commit to that.

Look at your calendar now and decide when you will do your decluttering. Will you do it for hours at a time? Will you break it up into ten-minute chunks? It doesn't matter. All that matters is making the time and following through. You can do it early before your kids wake up, on your lunch break, after you put your kids to bed, during nap time, on the weekend, whatever fits best (not easiest—best). However, I want to warn you of the temptation to do more and work longer, especially in the beginning when you're all inspired, full of momentum, and totally on a roll. Be careful not to run yourself into the ground! Don't derail your efforts by burning out too soon. Pace yourself. You've likely accumulated a lot of stuff over a lot of years. It's okay for this to take some time. The point is to find something that works for you and make slow, steady progress.

The key to succeeding is this: **prioritize your life.** This isn't extra. This doesn't fall into the "would be nice" category on your to-do list. This is important and it matters. Find the time and get it done, so you can literally create more time for what matters in your life. Show up for yourself and your family.

A lot of women tell me they just don't have the time. *You have the time.* I'd almost guarantee that you spend at least thirty minutes a day scrolling through social media. Treat this like an important appointment. If you really want to be able to have company over and not be embarrassed about your house, if you really want to be set free from the constant cycle of cleaning up all day, if you really want to have weekends that are spent having fun with your family instead of catching up on the laundry, then you've got to make it happen. If this was any other important appointment, you'd write it in your planner and show up prepared. Treat this the same way. We're creating a pattern here. Get intentional with this first step toward change, and it will pave the way for you to live a more intentional life for your family.

Maybe you'll have to make a sacrifice somewhere to fit this into your day. Do it. The return on investment is huge, because every time you finish a decluttering session, you'll have given yourself back minutes of the day that you didn't previously have. Remember, what takes up your space takes up your time.

Also remember that this is only temporary. You don't have to make the sacrifice forever. Just long enough to simplify your home, lighten your load, and make your life a whole lot better.

WHAT TO EXPECT

Let me toss you a pro tip: don't go into a room, gut it, throw everything on the floor, then start making decisions and sorting things into piles. All that's gonna do is overwhelm you even more and have you abandoning rooms with piles everywhere. What I want you to do in each room is simply pick up the first thing you see, look at it, and make a decision. Decide first, then put that item into a pile on the floor. This will keep you from pulling out everything you own and getting that "project overwhelm WTF did I do" feeling.

You should have three piles: keep, toss, and donate. That's it.

Now, I'm going to be honest with you. You're going to come across things that you'll feel incapable of making decisions about. The tiny white dress your daughter wore home from the hospital or the handmade quilt your grandmother gave you right before she passed away—you'll hold those items in your hands and feel totally stuck.

It's okay to feel overwhelmed by the decision-making process, but don't let it keep you from making progress. When you find yourself stuck on something sentimental or difficult, just set it aside or put it back for now. You'll have to deal with it eventually (I address it later in this book, and you'll be a total pro by then!), but you don't need to deal with it in the middle of a productive purging session.

Women are great multitaskers, but one thing I've seen totally derail someone's progress is starting in one area, seeing something that belongs in another area, moving it to its proper place, and then deciding to start purging that space instead of heading back to the original area. This is why I strongly encourage you *not* to put away your "keep" pile until you're done with the room you're currently working on. The name of the game is short spurts of massive progress in one area at a time!

When you're done with a room, *follow through with your piles.* You are not done with a decluttering session until you have followed it all the way through! Everything in your "keep" pile needs to be put in its new home. Everything in your "trash" pile needs to be bagged up and carried out to the garbage can. Everything in your "donate" pile needs to be bagged up and put in the back of your car for a trip to the

DECLUTTER LIKE A MOTHER

donation center. Once these things are done, you can check the box on your purge session for the day.

> **TIP:** Once you have donation items to drop off, look at your calendar for the next few days. When are you going to be heading out for soccer practice or an appointment? Set an alert to leave fifteen to thirty minutes early and take your items to the donation center on your way to what you've already planned to be out for.

CLUTTER IS A THIEF

One thing I know for sure is that clutter is much more than piles of hidden stuff you probably don't need. Clutter is a thief. It steals the space you're paying for, it steals your time, it steals your energy, it steals your mental clarity, it steals your joy. I've seen it straight up steal people's quality of life. On the surface, this all sounds pretty dramatic. But it's the truth. I've seen it over and over again, in my own life and in others'.

Here's the problem: most people's homes are working against them because of how they have them set up. They move into their homes, put a million appliances in the kitchen, put clothes they hate or don't wear in the closets, put books they'll never read on the shelves—they have too much stuff. So they stack boxes in the garage or in the attic and throw knick-knacks and odds and ends on the tops of dressers. The dining tables are no longer used for eating together as a family, but for spaces where they throw the stuff they don't know what to do with. They eat at the kitchen counter instead, which is littered with bills, school paperwork, and junk mail.

Sound familiar? If so, is that what you want? Is that the house you want to live in? Your home is supposed to be a safe space where memories are made. It's supposed to be a haven, a place where you can rest, recharge, be productive, and live well. Is your home set up in a way that makes this possible or makes this harder? Is your home a time and energy suck because of the layers of stuff you have to maintain?

Imagine a child pulling an empty wagon. He sees a rock, so he puts it in the wagon. No big deal because it doesn't really affect the weight of the wagon. He goes a little farther, sees another rock, picks it up, and puts it in the wagon. Again, not a huge deal. He can keep going pretty easily.

But what will happen if he keeps adding more rocks? Eventually the weight will become too much. He's going to get tired, his little arms are going to get weak, and he might give up. *Because the weight of the rocks is making it harder for him to do what he wants to do, which is to keep moving forward.*

The solution is simple: dump the rocks, kid! If he can't dump them all at once, he can at least remove them one at a time. Rock by rock, he can unload the wagon until it's lighter. It is the same with clutter. You need to dump out your clutter, girl. It's the rocks that are weighing you down.

Tell me if you often find yourself saying (read: yelling) these things:

- "Everything is such a mess!"
- "Come clean this up!"
- "Can't anyone help around here?"
- "Why do I have to do everything?"
- "Am I the only one with eyes that can see this mess?"

If this is you some, most, or even all the time (no judgment), it's a sign that your home isn't supporting you or working for you. It's actually working against you, because it's causing tension. It's causing all-around negativity in your home.

Sami Womack's story illustrates this in a way that you might relate to. She was one of the first five original students to enroll in my Your Uncluttered Home program back in 2016, and she completely changed the course of her family and her legacy as a mom. She generously agreed to share her story:

I would describe myself before this point in time as "desperate and drowning." My family and I were living beyond our means in a large, overstuffed house.

Every aspect of my life needed to be purged and downsized. This is when I found Allie. I did what she said and started with the house because the rest was just too overwhelming to do at the same time.

As I purged my home, I could feel brain space being freed up. Suddenly I could think straight.

The more stuff I got rid of, the lighter I felt. Time and energy I didn't know was even an option became available to me.

I feel like everything changed, but especially my relationship with my children. I can actually enjoy them. There's just not a lot of stress around my motherhood or my home. A few minutes of cleanup each day is all it takes.

People ask me all the time how I'm homeschooling and running a business with my husband gone half the time—it's the house. My house just does *not* take up much of my time or energy. That's saved for my kids.[6]

Clutter is a thief. For Sami, it stole her focus, her time, and her day-to-day happiness. Her home was set up to take from her. But she made the necessary changes so that her home was set up to work *for* her.

Before, Sami had stuff everywhere, which led to a lot of maintenance, stress, and time given to the house—resulting in less time for other things that were important to her. After completing the program, Sami had less stuff, which led to less maintenance, stress, and time given to the house—resulting in more time for other things that were important to her.

Let's look at what clutter is stealing from you. In 2016, a study led by a badass scientist named Catherine Roster found that "clutter had a negative impact on self-reported well-being and a 'strong negative impact on feelings of security, safety and other positive emotional benefits derived from a sense of psychological home,' a term that refers to the concept of 'home' as a 'vital source of meaning, belonging, and identity.'"[7]

Basically, **we have too much stuff, and it's stealing good things from us.** Not cool.

I must have received thousands of messages from women telling me that after they cleared the clutter out of one room, they just stood there for the longest time. Some even ended up eating their dinner in that room, because it felt so good and they didn't want to leave. This isn't random. It's science. A clear space literally lowers your cortisol. It feels good.

And my goal is for your entire house to feel like this. So get happy, girl.

A study by UCLA found that mothers use words like "mess," "not fun," and "very chaotic" to describe their homes. This is *so sad*. It's not supposed to be this way. And it definitely doesn't have to be. This is unnecessary stress and loss of value in life.

UCLA "looked at study participants' levels of diurnal cortisol [basically, they measured their stress] through saliva provided by the families. And they found that there did seem to be a link between how families, especially mothers, talk about their home spaces and their diurnal cortisol levels. . . . Thus, our excess becomes a visible sign of unaccomplished work that constantly challenges our deeply engrained notions of tidy homes and elicits substantial stress."[8]

I'll say it again: we are making our lives harder than they need to be. You're not a bad mom. You're just overwhelmed.

Of course it's too much! It's way too much for any one person to manage while still remaining calm, patient, present—all the makings of a "good mom."

How much stuff is sitting out on the surfaces of your home? How much is shoved in the drawers? If you got up and opened the nearest closet door, how much crap would you see? How many things do you have to maintain each day just to be able to live in your home? **We have put so much extra, unnecessary work on our plates.**

And the thing is, this is considered *normal*! Most Americans live in homes crammed with stuff. We move stuff around and put stuff away, stuff we don't even need—such as broken toys, clothes that don't fit, books we don't read, and gifts we didn't like when we opened them but somehow feel obligated to keep forever, like that horrific sweater from your Aunt Marg. *Why do we keep things like that? Why do we feel obligated to let something we don't like take up our space and time?*

We have too much of everything because we're afraid to make the decision to let go of anything. It all comes down to fear. Every single thing. Every single time. We don't want to let go of our stuff because we spent money on it (or someone else did), and we're afraid we'll feel guilty, or worse, selfish! We're afraid our spouses are going to get upset because we didn't keep that present they gave us for our birthday three years ago. We're afraid Grandma is going to ask why our kid isn't dressed in that baby outfit we kind of hate. We're afraid we're going to need something we haven't used in five years.

We're just afraid, and we're letting that fear stack up in a giant pile of unmade decisions. We're letting that fear decide how we live our lives. Yet, the thing we're most afraid of is happening right in front of us. **Because of our hesitance to kick fear in the butt and let go of the excess, we're literally missing out on our lives.**

"Isn't cleaning up all the time just a part of being a mom though? Isn't it just a sign of having kids?"

It is if you decide it is. Your reality will always follow your expectations. If you're buying into the belief that it's always going to be like this, that it's always harder because of the kids, then it will be.

I believe that I get to enjoy motherhood. I get to raise kids and live a beautiful life. Constant cleanup is not my penance for living my life.

My expectation is that things get to be good. I'm not available for constant chaos and constant messes that tie me to a to-do list. That affects the way I live, the things I allow into my space, and the way my home is set up. **My reality is following my expectations just like you.**

Obviously, if you have kids, your life and your home are going to look different from those of someone who doesn't. I'm not saying to set yourself up for unhappiness with insane expectations. I'm saying we don't have to subscribe to the "Hot Mess Mom" culture and accept the lie that once you have kids everything is a shit show.

So, no. Cleaning up all the time does not need to be a part of your life.

LET'S TALK ABOUT THIS IN TERMS OF MONEY

You're paying for every bit of square footage in your home. Is that space supporting the life you want, or is it working against that life? Is the space how you want it to look and feel based on how much time and money you spend on it?

How much money do you earn each month? I know what you're thinking: *Mind ya business, Allie.* I promise this is important though. And while we're at it, let me ask you these questions too (might as well get up close and personal, since you're about to let me in your closets anyway):

- What do you do for a living? Or what does your partner do for a living?
- What are all the ways money comes into your home?
- How much do you and/or your partner get paid an hour?
- How much of your product do you and/or your partner have to sell to meet your income goal for the month?
- How many hours a week do you and/or your partner have to work to earn your salary?

(*Side note:* If you're a stay-at-home mom, you're worth a billion and a half dollars. Like, per month. But I want you to look at the money that comes into your bank accounts right now.)

Crunch those numbers, girl! Got the number (or close to it) in your head? Of that amount, how much money do you spend on the place you live every month? A lot, right?

Whether you have a rent payment or a mortgage payment, most people spend the bulk of their money on their living space.

We all work for money. We all exchange time for money in some way. **No matter how you are making your money, your time is your money, and a big chunk of that money is going toward your home.**

So, what exactly are you paying for each month? It's not a trick question, but I'll give you the answer: square footage. You pay by square footage for the whole lot—the backyard, the bedrooms, the closets, the garage, the bathrooms, the basement, the attic, and so on.

Now, it's time for some honesty, friend. What percentage of that square footage—that you're paying for out of your hard-earned money—are you using to basically store stuff that you don't want, like, or need?

Do the math. Then really look at the numbers and let yourself feel that. Are you feeling uncomfortable? Panicked? Guilty? That's okay. Those feelings are going to lead to action if you let them.

Here's the thing, most people believe they're *intentionally* using all the space in their homes. They think they're being purposeful with their space because it's storing their stuff. But what stuff? Do you even know or remember or use or *care* about the stuff you're storing?

Look back at those numbers you just crunched. Is it worth it? What if you had a different perspective on your space and asked: "How can I make this square footage—that I'm paying for with hours of my life and dollar bills I earned—work for me, *with* me, and serve me and my family best?" If the answer isn't the way you're currently using it, then you need to make some changes.

So let's get down to the nitty-gritty. Do you like your home? Do you like what you see and feel when you walk in? I'm not asking if you like your family. I'm asking about the inside of your actual house. Do you even like it? Is it working for you or against you?

We think we're okay because "everyone is doing it." This thinking is doing nothing but giving us a false sense of security. Our biggest fear is happening by our own hands and our own choices. This self-talk is a form of self-sabotage. We're squandering so many beautiful moments, because, remember, what takes up our space takes up our time.

When we say yes to keeping our junk, we're saying no to feeling peace in our own homes. When we say yes to constantly having to clean and maintain, we're saying no to doing something purposeful or enjoyable. When we say yes to crashing into bed at night because we're so freaking tired from dealing with the stress and mess all day, we're saying no to an evening with our partners or an evening to ourselves! When we say yes to not being ruthless editors of our homes, we're saying no to enjoying the space we work so hard to pay for.

You don't have to keep saying yes to the things that aren't serving you. You don't have to drown in your stuff. You don't have to keep fighting to keep your head above the water. I know because I kicked and paddled and swam my way to shore, and now I'm coming back for you. I have the lifeline, and I'm standing here on solid ground tossing it to you. I'm ready to pull you in. All you have to do is grab hold. All you have to do is say "no more."

When you say no to the excess, no to the extra work, no to more cleaning, no to more stress, no to more mess, no to more yelling, no to more nagging, you are automatically saying yes to the right things, to the important things. You're saying yes to more snuggling on the couch with your sweetheart, to more playing LEGO with your kids, to more alone time, to more enjoying the house that you live in.

That's the whole purpose of this book. That's the whole purpose of this lifestyle change. It isn't about having a "perfect" house. It isn't about having photo-ready home decor. It isn't about how much money you have. This is about you and your family. This is about functionality and the way you are spending your days. Annie Dillard said, "How we spend our days is, of course, how we spend our lives."[9]

If you're spending all day running around like a chicken with your head cut off, cleaning all the time, and never enjoying your life, your house isn't functioning *well*. In fact, I would say it isn't functioning *at all*. It's *malfunctioning*.

As I've already mentioned, this is about much more than having a clean home. This is about taking back what our clutter is stealing from us. This is about moving against the status quo and deciding to clear the way for a life we can be present for.

This passes on to generations still to come. I don't want my death to come with the added burden for my kids to have to sort through rooms and layers and drawers and boxes full of stuff no one needs. I don't want my kids to take time out of their lives to sort through what I avoided while also grieving.

I want my kids to know there is a better way to live than mindlessly buying stuff you don't need and shoving it in closets and hidden spaces until you die. I don't want them to settle for what is "normal" for everyone else. I don't want junk getting passed from closet to closet with every move. I don't want to show my children that this is how I treat myself and my space. I want to give them the freedom of less—not only now as they are growing up, but as a model of how to live when they're adults with their own homes.

This is a gift you give your family. This shifts the legacy you leave behind. This matters. Status quo isn't good enough for your family. Let's move beyond it.

THREE

HOW MINIMALISM CAN STEAL YOUR JOY (AND HOW TO STAY HAPPY INSTEAD)

WHAT WE'RE DOING HERE IS CREATING A SPACE THAT aligns with how you want to feel in your home. But if you're not careful, you can fall into soul-sucking minimalism traps.

Instead of giving you the joy and freedom that you so desperately desire, this lifestyle of minimalism that seems like an oasis can turn into quicksand fast. I can't tell you how many times I've seen trendy, stereotypical minimalism suck the joy right out of people's lives. They give up their decision-making power and get lost in a life of counting and rule-following—counting jeans, counting shoes, counting books. Life becomes all about keeping the amount of possessions they own under a certain number. It becomes about following the rules some minimalist teacher somewhere told them they had to follow in order to be a "minimalist."

These people are missing the point of simplifying by obsessing over the details and the numbers. It's *so easy* to do. They're exchanging the handcuffs their stuff shackled them with for a new set of shiny handcuffs gifted to them by "minimalist rules." They're still giving power and energy to their stuff—in a new way.

The point of all of this is to make the process work for you, not for you to follow someone else's rules. Throughout this book, I'll be giving you helpful suggestions and tips by pushing you to let go of the things that are taking up too much of your time and aren't worth it. But please know that you can and should "keep the meat and throw out the bones" as you read. Not everything in this book is for everyone. I want you to be empowered to tweak, adjust, and create a space you love with me as your guide, not as your drill sergeant.

SIGNS YOU'RE LETTING MINIMALISM STEAL YOUR JOY

It's important to find a balance as you go through your home and get rid of items. Although it will likely be tiresome and emotional at times, it should not leave you feeling joyless but satisfied and hopeful. Here are some red flags that minimalism is taking its toll on your joy.

1. YOU FIND YOURSELF STALLING AND PROCRASTINATING INSTEAD OF TAKING ACTION BECAUSE YOU'RE AFRAID YOU'LL "DO IT WRONG." I see a lot of women getting stuck here. You google *minimalism*, and

you see perfect homes, perfect closets, perfect kids. Perfect, perfect, perfect. You compare, and before you know it you've compared yourself right out of action. Let me say it again in case you haven't totally grasped it yet—forget the rules! There are no rules. And if there are, they aren't for us. You don't have to worry about "doing it wrong" for one more second. There is no wrong way; there is only your way. And your way is the best way. And guess what? It's okay to grow and evolve through this process, circling back to go deeper and declutter more as you learn. It doesn't all have to be done in the first round.

2. YOU MAYBE, SORT OF, BUT DEFINITELY OBSESS OVER HOW SOMEBODY ELSE DOES THIS. I get messages all the time from women who are in the decluttering process and want to know exactly how many towels I have, or how many pairs of shoes I keep for my kids, or how much makeup I own. Hear me when I say it really doesn't matter what I do.

Don't obsess over how someone else does this. I encourage you to figure out what works for you, your family, and your lifestyle.

How many times a week do you want to do the laundry? How many people live in your house? What sort of weather do you deal with where you live? These are things that will change person to person, and you'll need to find your own sweet spot. You'll need to learn to identify when you have too much of something in your space. You'll need to become very aware of how it annoys you, how much space it takes up, and how much better you'd feel if it were less (or gone).

For now, just keep reading and remember, there are no rules, only helpful and less helpful ways to do this.

3. YOU LOOK FOR A WAY THIS WON'T WORK FOR YOU, INSTEAD OF BEING OPEN-MINDED AND WILLING TO GIVE IT A TRY. Why not just try it? What's the worst that can happen? Better question: What's the *best* thing that can happen?

4. YOU FEEL GUILTY KEEPING THINGS YOU LOVE. YOU ALWAYS FEEL LIKE YOU COULD, AND SHOULD, GET RID OF MORE. You look over your jewelry, and you just know you don't want to get rid of anything. All your necklaces and earrings express who you are and you love them, but you hear a voice in your head telling you: "They're just not worth your time," or "You have too many."

That voice isn't yours. It's the voice of legalistic minimalism. Instead of tuning it out and doing what feels good for you, you listen and feel guilty for keeping those earrings you love because you're sure a "true minimalist" would never have this much jewelry.

5. YOU EXPECT DECLUTTERING TO BE A ONE-AND-DONE EVENT INSTEAD OF A PROCESS. You're human, and a beautiful thing about humans is that we evolve and grow. The decisions you make during your initial purge may not always serve you or your lifestyle. Your needs and wants may change. Your job may change. Your family may change. You may find that you will need to purge again, and this time you may make different decisions than the ones you made last time. That's okay. It's all a part of this new lifestyle. Expect to do maintenance purges along the way.

6. YOU FEEL GUILT OVER THE AMOUNT OF MONEY YOU'VE WASTED ON YOUR STUFF, INSTEAD OF LETTING THE REALIZATION MAKE YOU A MORE MINDFUL CONSUMER. Focus on what I'm about to say: the wasting of money doesn't happen by removing what's no longer useful to you; it

happens when you buy something you don't need. Write that on a Post-It note and stick it wherever you'll see it daily if you need to. This is the mindset shift you need to make.

When you first start purging, you're going to realize how much money you're tossing into your "donate" or "trash" piles. Don't let this trip you up and keep you from moving forward. Allow the realization to come, accept it, and choose to let it be a catalyst for change.

It may be difficult, but it needs to happen to make you a more mindful consumer. The realization of how wasteful you've been in the past will make you want to stop contributing to the problem of consumeristic waste in the world. It will teach you lessons that will serve you, your family, and the world as a whole. It's okay to have made mistakes. Learning from them is what's important.

One of my favorite quotes from Maya Angelou applies well here: "Forgive yourself for not knowing what you didn't know before you learned it."

Learn the lesson, be grateful for it, and move on.

7. YOU BELIEVE YOU CAN NEVER SHOP OR PURCHASE ANYTHING AGAIN. This is another big way I've seen minimalism steal joy from people. On a tough mom day, isn't it nice to take a break from the kids, grab a coffee, and walk through Target? You don't have to stop doing things like that! But you do need to start asking yourself *why* you're doing them. There's nothing wrong with browsing the aisles, getting home inspiration, and maybe even leaving with some items that will make your space happier or more functional.

However, some people shop primarily to fill an inner void

instead of shopping to supply a physical need. The next time you find yourself at Target or browsing your favorite shopping app, ask yourself if you're shopping to fill a void or to fill a need.

Do you find yourself only shopping when you've had a bad day? Or has your body shifted or your style changed, and so you just need some new wardrobe pieces? There's nothing wrong with purchasing things to make you feel confident or to make your home look beautiful. Just be aware of your motives. **Minimalism doesn't need to be the end of your shopping, just the end of mindless consuming.**

I recorded and released an episode "How Minimalism Can Steal Your Joy" on my podcast, *The Purpose Show*, that can help you with this further. To listen, go to alliecasazza .com/joy.

Like anything designed to help you make life changes, if you turn minimalism into a set of rules based on a philosophy that you must follow to a T, it very quickly loses its ability to give you the freedom you're looking for.

Are you asking questions like:

- What are the rules?
- How many books should I have?
- How many pairs of jeans do I keep?
- What about underwear? How many is too many?

If so, you are missing the point. You are looking for a set of rules to follow, and I've rarely seen this kind of legalistic minimalism work for moms. The process of decluttering has to go deeper than that. It has to be less about keeping a perfect home and more about being freed up to live your life.

I've always viewed this lifestyle as one that can help me be the mom and person I want to be. That's the heart of the method for me. And it works! That's why my message has reached people in Russia, China, Australia, and parts of the world I'd never heard of. That's why people are talking about it. It works *for* you.

So don't obsess over the rules, or the details, or the numbers. Don't wait for permission; instead take ownership. Minimalism is a tool. Let it help you remove what's weighing you down and make space for life to happen.

This is about more space in your home, more breathing room to rest and enjoy and live. It's about less yelling, less stress, less fighting with your family to just clean the eff up. It's removing the need for organization, because you don't need to rearrange your junk; you need to let go of it. It's less crap in your way, less on your to-do list, and more checks on your bucket list. It's more "feel good" moments with your family. Isn't that what you want?

Life is waiting to be lived. Consider how much joy and time your stuff has already stolen from you. Let the weight of that realization sink in, feel the emotions, maybe even get a little mad about it, then take action. It's time to take back your life and make your space work for you rather than against you.

Let's do this.

FOUR

LET'S GET IT STARTED IN HERE! (NAILED THE FERGIE IMPRESSION, LIKE I ALWAYS DO)

YOU'VE GOT THE FOUNDATION DOWN NOW. WE'VE COV-ered the basics, and it's time to get into the nitty-gritty of purging. I'm about to drop two key pieces of knowledge you're going to need before you get at it. These two components are the basis for successfully decluttering each room in your house. Ready?

The first thing I need you to understand is something you're going to do *internally* for each room in your home. This is going to make the process of physically decluttering much easier for you. It's going to give you an internal benchmark for saying yes or no to items as you sort. This is why it's so important not to gloss over this step. I call it *setting the intent.*

SET THE INTENT FOR EACH ROOM

Let's play the imagination game again. Picture this: you walk into a room, your mom outfit is on point, you're rocking the top knot, you've got trash bags in each hand, and you're feeling energized. It's game time, baby, and you are in the zone. You look around the room and take it all in.

Instead of immediately picking up the first thing you see, ask yourself: What is my vision for this room? I want you to hold space for it, and really question how the room can serve you and your family. What do you need out of this space? What do you need it to do for you?

If you need some clarity, here are some questions you can ask yourself:

- Do I like how I'm using this room right now? Is it working for me?
- What do I want this room to be used for? Don't limit your answer to the traditional use for your rooms. Is there some out-of-the-box idea that you've had for this space but felt like it was too weird? You do you, girl! It's your home! Your name is on that rent or mortgage check. You can do whatever you want to make that space work for you!
- How do I want to feel when I'm in this room?
- How do I want my family to feel?
- How do I want guests to feel? (Obviously, we probably don't need to think about this question when we're setting the intent for our bedrooms. Or maybe you do. No judgment here.)

- What are some practical things I could do to this space to make it simpler, easier, and happier?
- Who am I in this room? (I'm going to clarify this one in a minute.)

Your answers to these questions will lead to your intent for each space. They will determine so much of what you keep or don't keep in those rooms.

For example, I don't love cooking. My husband, Brian, does most of the cooking in our home, and he keeps it pretty simple. We don't have a lot of extra gadgets and cooking utensils. We just have the essentials: a set of high-quality pots and pans, spatulas, and other basic cookware. Because we don't love to cook or spend excessive amounts of time in the kitchen, we want that room to be simple and clean. We want to have what we need and the things we have to be easy to put away.

My friend Jess, on the other hand, loves to cook. She's basically a chef. Williams Sonoma gift cards are her love language. The kitchen is her happy place, and she's just creative in there. Who she is in her kitchen is very different from who I am in mine; so her kitchen is going to look different from mine. This is what I mean by asking the question: Who am I in this room?

This relativity applies to any space. Let's look at another example. If I were a lawyer, my office would have a certain look. I might have a big bookcase filled with books about law (I obviously don't know much about being a lawyer, but let's go with that), a desk with plenty of space, and extra chairs for clients. My office would have a certain intent, a certain objective, based on who I am in that room.

But I'm not a lawyer. I'm an online business owner, and I deal with home and motherhood. I also love a pretty space, and my office is the setting for most of the videos I film, so you'll see my touch in the details that matter to me. The intent for my office is completely different from that of a lawyer.

Let's move to the bedroom. I'm married, so I have an extra-large bed. (Why is this paragraph feeling awkward?) My intent for this room is to have a space for self-care and rest for both me and my husband. Our room reflects who we are and what we need to bookend our days. Our bedside tables each hold what we need and nothing more. Mine always has the book I'm currently reading, Chapstick, moisturizer, and a salt-rock lamp for that soothing nighttime glow.

This is a space where I begin and end my days. I also practice my morning ritual in this room, so it's important to me that I enjoy being here and can wind down as well as gear up for the day. (For more about my morning ritual, go to alliecasazza.com/morningritual.)

The intent you set for your bedroom may require you to keep different things in there than I keep in mine. If you're a single mom working two jobs, your bedroom needs to be a place just for you, a place where you can turn off the world and fall into a restful and rejuvenating sleep. Maybe you don't want a television in there; maybe you do. Maybe you want a lot of candles and oils; maybe you don't. Maybe you want a lot of decor to make you happy; maybe having no decor is what calms you. Whatever you need to help you show up for your purpose is what you should have taking up space in your bedroom. **Set the intent.**

If you look around your room and see something stored in your closet that really makes you feel stressed—like a filing cabinet—you need to get that out. That filing cabinet has no business taking up space, giving you paperwork vibes, and causing stress in the very room where you're restoring yourself. If you don't ask yourself who you are in your bedroom and how you need it to support you, you'll keep that cabinet in there because that's where it's always been. We want to stop the autopilot and be intentional.

Setting the intent for each room is so important, which is why it's the first step in this journey. It will help you decide what to keep and what to move out of each space.

How to Set the Intent When It's Not Really Your Space

There are some spaces in your home that are not totally yours. For those, you'll have to work with other family members to set the intent. Places like your kid's room or a general family area like the loft or the game room. These are rooms where you're not the only person using them, so it won't feel good for everyone else if you are the only one deciding what to keep. So, how do you set the intent for these areas?

Make it a family thing! Invite family members into the decision-making process with you (if they're old enough). If it's a room your child spends time in, and they're over the age of four, ask them to help you decide how to best use the room. I've provided a list of great questions (and follow-up questions) to help get your kids' wheels turning when it comes to setting the intent for their space.

- How do you feel when you're in this room? Happy? Safe? Scared?
- Does this room make you smile?
- Do you like how this room looks right now? No? How would you like it to look?
- How would you like this room to feel? Peaceful? Fun? Calm? Exciting?
- Is there anything in here you like?
- Is there anything in here you don't like?

Ask your kids. Have the conversation. Obviously, you don't have to do anything crazy like putting in a slide (although that would be amazing). The point is to just check in with them. I think we sometimes forget that we can actually have conversations with our kids about the day-to-day things they experience. It doesn't have to be the way it's always been, and they'll appreciate that you care.

Use your adult logic here too. Do your kids have books thrown everywhere? Add a bookcase or shelves on the wall. Are you noticing anything about their room that's not lining up with who your child is? Make the space fit them more. For example, if your child is an introvert who needs time alone to recharge but there's no space for them in their room to relax and regroup, then change it.

I had a woman message me once, thanking me for teaching her how to set the intent for her kid's room. She walked through these questions with her five-year-old and figured out that he was scared of a poster that had been hanging in there for *years*. He just didn't know to tell her that until she asked.

They removed the poster and put up one that he likes, and now his room makes him happy and he likes being in there.

By asking these questions, we're reconfiguring the layout of our homes and the stuff in our rooms. We're rethinking the systems that have naturally developed as we've been doing life day in and day out on autopilot. By asking whether what we've been doing is working out or not, we're taking a step back and being intentional.

When it comes to spaces that belong to your partner or that you're sharing with your partner, have an honest conversation with them. Communicate how you're feeling about the house and what you're trying to do. Explain how the two of you spend most of your income on your home, and how you think it could work well for the entire family.

Ask how they want the space to feel. Share how you want the space to feel. Find some common ground and compromise. Don't try to control them or the situation. Just be honest and communicate. Who knows? They might be feeling and wanting the same things. Even if they've never thought about it, and the clutter does not bother them, most people want to live in a happy space with a happy partner.

IDENTIFY THE CLUTTER CRUTCH

If you're like most people, there may be a space in your home where things go to die, whether it's an entire floor, one room, or a Monica Gellar–style secret closet. It is our hidden beast. I call it the clutter crutch.

One of our biggest goals in life is to make sure that guests never find or see this space. It's the holding cell for all your unmade decisions. It's that "extra" space where you throw things and quickly shut the door. Heck, it might even be the entire house itself (I've seen this, and you are not alone), so you never invite anyone over. No matter where your clutter crutch is, lift your head up, because we're about to tackle this monster and send him packing.

The problem with having a clutter crutch is that while you're decluttering like a mother, you always have a fallback, a safety net in which to throw things you're indecisive about. You'll be decluttering—but not really. You'll just be moving your crap from one room to another, which is not progress. And we really want to make progress!

Having a clutter crutch keeps messes alive and well in your home. Stacking your stuff in spaces like this increases stress in your mind. In the end, one of two things is going to happen:

1. You're eventually going to have to deal with it—get in there and make the decisions. And it will likely take much longer, because you kept piling stuff in there while working through the other rooms.
2. You're going to leave it—close the door and try to forget about it. But it will always be in the back of your mind, which is way worse because it will continue to bother you.

So, let's start by calling that space in your house what it is: a clutter crutch. What does yours look like? Picture it in your mind. Where is it? Is it big or small? Do you have more than one? Get a clear image.

The good news is, I'm not going to have you tackle that space right now. It's not the time. We'll deal with it together in chapter 10. What's important now is being aware of the clutter crutch and promising me and yourself that whatever you do, you won't add stuff to it as you go through your other rooms. The endless, mindless cycle of throwing things in this space, adding to the monster pile, and closing the door ends right now.

So far in this chapter, I've unloaded two things you are going to need to know before you grab those trash bags and get at it. The first was setting the intent for your spaces, and the second was identifying the clutter crutch and promising not to add to it through this process.

With these two pieces of knowledge, you now know what to do first in each space and what you need to watch out for. You have the beginning guide that will help you make progress. Now it's time to get going and actually work through specific rooms.

And I know exactly where you should start: where poop happens.

FIVE

BEGIN HERE: WHERE POOP HAPPENS

GIRL, THIS IS IT. THE NITTY-GRITTY.

We're starting in the bathrooms. And I would suggest starting in *your* bathroom.

A lot of people don't want to start in the bathroom. They're all inspired, they feel gung-ho, and they want to start somewhere that seems like it will make more of an impact, like the kitchen or their kids' rooms. You can for sure do whatever you want, but if I were there with you in person, I'd make sure we start in the bathroom.

The reason is this: the bathroom is an easy "yes or no" area. It's much easier to make decisions about old makeup and broken hair tools than about a sentimental box of valuables from your grandmother. And unless you have a really funky way of storing things in your house, you're not going to find sentimental things in this room.

When we start with the easiest decisions, we get on a roll and are able to build momentum that we will need for the rest of the house. So by starting in the bathroom, you're setting yourself up for your most successful start.

Maybe you only have one bathroom and everyone in your house shares it. Maybe you have several bathrooms and you each have your own. Or maybe you have enough bathrooms, but somehow everyone always ends up in yours. It doesn't really matter what your bathroom situation is; the process will be pretty much the same across the board.

Remember, don't try to change the way your family uses your home; just know *how* it gets used and declutter in a way that it becomes easier and more enjoyable to use.

Bathrooms are kind of junk city. There is so much stuff that ends up shoved in bins and drawers wrapped with hairs and dental floss. Ew. Let's go over a few things that are likely crammed in this space:

lotions	flat iron
dental floss	curling iron
pads	dry shampoo (#lifesaver)
tampons	foundation
random toothbrush from that dentist visit two years ago	primer
	concealer
	eyeshadows
body spray	lash curlers
hair sprays	powder blush
hairbrush	cream blush
bobby bins	lip colors
hair clips	mascaras
hair dryer	makeup brushes

makeup removers	waxing kits
razors	loofahs
shaving cream	bodywash
bandages	deodorant
Neosporin	mouthwash
aloe vera	contact solution
sunscreen	jewelry
empty medicine bottles	cleaners
extra pregnancy tests	books
lubricants	magazines
birth control	candles
dried-up bars of soap	paper towels
Q-tips	bath toys
cotton balls	washcloths
nail polish	hand towels
nail polish remover	bath towels
tweezers	dirty clothes

Phew! This list isn't even exhaustive! It's ridiculous, honestly.

I'm Allie Casazza. Minimalism is literally my job, and I still get tripped up in this black-hole room of the house! The other day I was looking for my hair-scrunching spray. I was going through my bathroom cabinets looking for it, and I thought, *Oh my gosh. I've done it again. There's so much under here.*

Now, do you remember the best way to start decluttering any room? Set the intent.

I know what you're thinking: *Allie, I get that, but this tip seems way too intense for purging my old nail polishes. Pretty sure you need to relax.*

No way, girl. We have to set the intent in *every* room!

In a place like the bathroom, some questions you might ask yourself to dig deeper into your intent might be:

- What do I use this room for? (This is where my kids would yell "pooping!" and crack themselves up. But I want you to get deeper than that.)
- How do I want to feel when I'm in here? Or, how do I want my guests or family members to feel when they're in here?
- What are some practical things I can have in this space to make it simpler, easier to use, and happier to come into?

Maybe you'll begin to see that every space in your home has a deeper purpose than you originally realized, and that there are things you can do to serve your family, yourself, and your guests better—thus making your home a true haven!

For example, I created a tiny oasis of beauty and amenities in our super-small guest bathroom downstairs. I started by setting the intent for the space. I wanted people to come into that room (after asking the awkward question, "Where's the restroom?") and enter a space where everything is ready for them. Where they have everything they need and feel welcome in our home, even if they need to poop. If they realize they need feminine hygiene products, they're in there. If they need to freshen up the space after using the toilet, there are several room sprays to choose from. There would always be extra toilet paper, flushable wipes, organic candles, matches—all the little amenities one could need in a guest bathroom.

I installed a pretty storage basket above the toilet where I keep the said amenities, plus Q-tips, lotion, and other items visitors might need. There's a pretty, squishy rug on the floor, and an indoor plant in a gorgeous ceramic pot. There's also a letter-board sign that reads HAVE A NICE POOP to bring a little humor and help people relax. (To watch a little video tour of my super-small guest bathroom, go to alliecasazza .com/mybathroom.)

The main bath upstairs is a space for me and my husband only, since it's in our bedroom. I wanted to make sure we were as taken care of as our guests. It's so easy to make sure our guest and living areas are life-giving and beautiful, but then leave our own spaces with no personal touches. Don't do this!

The intent I set for our bathroom was one of rest and peace. I love bubble baths, so candles line the tub in a cozy but not cluttered way. I have a large bohemian-style rug that takes up the entire tile floor, making it cozy to step out of the bath or shower. Our towels are extra plush, I have a massive terry cloth bathrobe hanging on a beautiful metal hook on the door, and my favorite organic body scrub (it smells like vanilla!) is in the shower ready to exfoliate and relieve my stressed-out body.

There are lots of ways to get yourself excited about each and every room, even the bathrooms. By setting the intent for this space, you build inspiration within yourself and realize that this process matters. It gives you some momentum to clear the clutter—all the crap that's keeping this space from feeling the way you want it to feel!

The next step is to simply dive in. Don't get stuck in a perfection mentality before you even begin. Choose one bathroom in your house and dive in with the attitude that you're going to get done what you're able to get done. We are looking for progress over perfection. Just start!

When it comes to tackling a new project, it can feel like a lot. It often feels overwhelming to approach simplicity. Ironic, I know. Clear the brain clutter that comes with starting something new by focusing on just thirty minutes a day. Spend thirty minutes in one area and see what you can accomplish!

Perfection would say: "I have to do the bathroom today. I don't know what I'm doing, but I have to do it all right now." Progress isn't about that. Simply focus for thirty minutes on getting rid of what you don't use or don't need and see what happens. Don't push yourself into a panic. Don't freak yourself out trying to be perfect. The all-or-nothing mentality is the absolute killer of productivity. I feel like you should highlight that.

The first step in decluttering your bathroom is to clear the visual clutter. For example, if all you see when you walk into your bathroom are your kids' bath toys, that is visual clutter.

BATH TOYS

Gather the toys up and ask yourself: *What do they actually play with?* Depending on your kids' ages, likes, and dislikes, you might be able to choose just a couple of toys and get rid of the rest. Older kids might want a toy shark or a hot wheel to play with. If you have little ones and want to keep a bigger selection for them, you can store the toys in a cute mold-resistant bin that you can stick to the side of the tub. (You can buy them at Target or on Amazon.) The main thing is to only keep what they really use. Everything else can be tossed.

Most mamas reading this feel bad about throwing out their kids' toys, so there is often an overabundance. It feels wasteful to get rid of perfectly nice toys. Let me speak some truth to you: it is not wasteful. **Keeping things you don't use is wasteful.** It's wasting your time and your space and your energy.

Visualization is also a big part of making the bathroom work for you. Sure, the purpose of a bathroom is pretty functional, but how can we function well when we're overwhelmed by what we see every time we open the door?

Be brave, mama. Toss the toys. Now your kids can get in the bath, play with the few toys they actually like to play with, and easily put them away when bath time is over.

Also, keep in mind that your kids can put their own toys away. It may take some time, but eventually they'll learn that putting their toys away is just what they do. This is a great teaching opportunity with your kids that can help them the rest of their lives!

Here's an example from my own life: My parents have a pool and my kids love to swim at Mimi and Papi's house. They live just down the road from us, so we go there nearly every day in the summer. There is a vacuum at the bottom of the pool that turns on automatically when we're done swimming.

My kids have all kinds of pool toys that sink to the bottom and know to dive after them before the vacuum starts. They know that if they leave their toys at the bottom of the pool, they will get sucked up and break the vacuum, which is an expensive repair. The kids know this, so they never leave their toys at the bottom of the pool. We, of course, remind them of this. But they've learned to do it even when we don't remind them, because they know that's not how we treat our things. We've set a precedent over time, and they know to follow it.

If you make something a rule or set a precedent in your home—if you say, "Hey, this is the way things work"—over time, kids will naturally do it. It's not magic. Kids don't just magically care, but eventually they will do it because they know this is how living in your house works. Just because they're young doesn't mean they don't have the ability to develop and follow through on habits that help you and your home function smoothly.

Speaking of rules—let's call them guidelines instead, since that's really what they are—set a hard one for the hot-mess bathroom space: if you haven't used the item in the last thirty days, it is not something you should hold on to.

MAKEUP

It's normal to be drawn to more stuff. All you have to do is walk down the aisle at Target and see that Kristin Ess has a new line out, and it's all over. Because, obviously, you need one of everything.

If my mom was reading an article in a magazine and there was a page dedicated to Jennifer Aniston's Oscar Red Carpet makeup look, she would tear out the page and go buy the look. It doesn't even have to be a look my mom would ever wear; the magazine just made her feel like she had to have it. And where does that stuff end up? Yep. The bathroom.

You know what has always kind of baffled me? This room is such a private area in a woman's life, yet people always seem to gift us things that belong in this room. Ya know? It's like, "Merry Christmas! Here's a $12 bottle of lotion to rub on your body."

"Thanks, Uncle Joe . . ."

And you keep it because someone spent $12 on it, or you think maybe you can gift it to someone else. Just stop. Break the body-rub-gift-giving cycle. I mean, it's no wonder the bathroom is a total circus.

Besides the fact that if you haven't used it in the last month, and you probably won't, almost everything that you keep in your bathroom has an expiration date. It can be hard to throw makeup away. I get it. Makeup isn't cheap. Even drugstore makeup can be expensive. *Dear Popular Makeup Brand, why does your mascara that is made out of God-only-knows-what and comes off the second a drop of sweat leaves my face cost $12.99?*

But keeping old makeup is really unsanitary. It actually collects microbes over time. *Gross.* Let the fact that your eyeshadow is literally collecting bacteria be the reason you toss it in the trash.

Too often we hold on to items we don't use or that are way past their expiration date because we *might* use it *one day.*

Or because it feels too wasteful. Or . . . we could snap out of it, realize we're not Taylor Swift and this glitter eyeshadow and hot-red lipstick isn't our look, and let it go.

Once you've thrown away all the old, expired makeup, lay out the rest of your beauty products on your counter. Take an honest look through these products and ask yourself what you actually wear every day. What do you use for your daily look? If you're a stay-at-home mom, and most days you're makeup-free and your mom bun is being held together with dry shampoo (been there), consider what you actually use whenever you do put yourself together. Whether that's for Sunday church or Saturday date night or some other event, what do you really use on a regular basis?

I'm not talking about makeup for a special event like a charity gala. I'm talking about products that you use on a more regular basis. What makes you up as a person when you go out somewhere? That's you. That's your look. Those are the products you keep. Maybe there's an exception, like a great red lipstick you don't use every day but like how it makes you feel, and so you have it as a special-event lip color. You can keep that if you know you will continue to use it periodically, and it's not past its expiration date.

Next up, let's talk about your obsession.

YOUR SECRET GROOMING OBSESSION

Every bathroom dweller has a secret grooming obsession. It's that one thing you can't not pick up when you're in Target.

Mine is nail polish. That's always been my thing. For whatever reason, when my nails are painted, I feel like I must be doing okay, like I'm put together. So I'd been collecting my favorite brand of nail polish like they were going out of business. I wasn't using all of them. I just had them.

A few years ago when I had a little bit of a tighter budget, I would do my own nails. But now, I get my nails done every couple of weeks by a gem of a human named Lucia. When I first started having my nails professionally done, I still kept buying nail polish. I had two plastic storage drawers full of about twenty nail polish colors and cuticle pushers and other nail supplies.

One day, I was in my bathroom going through my drawers and saw all these polishes I didn't use anymore. I realized that these were no longer a part of who I am, and I needed to let them go. I did keep the cuticle pushers and a couple of different colored polishes, so if I'm in a spot and needed to paint my own nails, I could. But the rest of it I chucked. If I had decided to stubbornly hold on to all those colors just in case *someday* I started doing my own nails again, you know what? They'd probably all be globby and expired anyway. Better to share them now with someone who will use and enjoy them while they're relatively fresh. I got rid of all the excess, and now I have so much space when I open my cabinets. It feels amazing. **As I changed as a person, my space changed to match.**

What's your obsession item? What product do you have in oversupply? This is the item that if the world ever ran out of it, they could easily come and grab some inventory from your cabinets. What are you always drawn to and tend to buy when you see it?

Let me offer another helpful guideline. When you're faced with more than three of anything, invoke the rule of numbers to help you make decisions: **Keep two of your favorites and declutter the rest.**

Now, if this part of the process is painful for you, if you can't imagine tossing all your lip colors because you change your look a lot, it's okay. I get that. I have a tip for that too: the rule of space. Collect all of them and dedicate a spot or a drawer for organizing trays. Tell yourself and everyone listening that this is the space where you're going to keep this item—but when it gets full, you'll have to declutter. I do this with my lip colors, and it works great.

I have a drawer in my bathroom that is sectioned off with plastic trays. There's a tray for my face products like foundation and primer, a tray for my eyes (shadows, liner, mascara), and a tray for my lips. In the tray for my lips, there's only space for about ten lip colors. I have colors for date nights. I have happy colors that pop just so, which I wear when filming. I also have things I use every day like lip balms and neutral lip colors. But that tray is my rule, my limit. And when it's full, then I'm tapped out of lip colors.

If the rule of numbers is too hard for you, I get it. Just remember, this isn't about only having a certain number of mascaras. This is about filling your space with things you actually use.

The next area of the bathroom we're going to look at is the shower.

SHOWER

Go look at what's in there. What do you use? Do you have a bunch of half-used body washes or razors? Toss them! You only need one good one—you don't need multiples. Keep one sharp razor, one conditioner, one loofah or washcloth, and one face wash. Which one do you always grab for? That's the one you keep. Get rid of the rest.

Perhaps you're budget minded and buy body wash in bulk, because you know you'll use it when you run out. That's okay. Store it under the sink or somewhere nearby but out of sight. You don't have to get rid of things unnecessarily if you know you're going to use them before they expire. The goal is to get multiples out of your line of vision. You only need to have one of each thing in the shower with you. Otherwise, it's cluttered. It's not relaxing. It's just visual clutter, which we all know at this point kills our vibe.

Remember the intent you set for this space! It probably didn't involve visual clutter and a feeling of stress.

LET'S DO IT

Now that we've gone over specific items and areas that need to be decluttered, let's start using the steps of decluttering: sort, toss, organize, put away. Normally, you won't have a donate pile for the bathroom, since most of the items have probably been used or expired, and that's not good for anybody.

When you start decluttering, you're essentially sorting

things into piles. So, clear a space on your floor for making piles. Then, open a drawer and start. I'm going to remind you again: don't get stuck in perfectionism. Just open a drawer and begin by making that first decision.

If you decide to keep an item, put it in your Keep pile. If you decide to toss an item, put it in your Toss pile. If it belongs somewhere else in the house, put it in the Put Away pile. I recommend using an empty laundry basket for this last pile. That way you can throw everything in there that goes somewhere else, and when you're finished, you can carry it around to the other rooms and put items back where they belong.

The other day, I actually found a cat toy and a coffee mug under my sink. *Why?* Stuff constantly surrounds us, and sometimes it comes into our homes without us even realizing it, like the cat toy. I don't remember ever seeing it before; yet, there it was, shoved in my bathroom. Decluttering should be an everyday part of life, and that's why it's a great habit to form now!

TIP: When sorting, let dust be your guide. Any bottle with a dusty coating on the lid should probably automatically go in the trash. Do you know how long it takes for an item to collect dust when it's under a cabinet? Answer: *a while.* No saying "Oh, now that I found this, I'll use it." No, you won't ever use it, and you know it! I'm on to you.

You also don't need to keep anything that's broken. Fraying toothbrushes, combs with missing teeth, makeup brushes with no handle—those are all things that can be tossed. This is where you might notice things that need to be replaced. Keep a pen and notepad handy (or open a Note on your phone), and write down anything you need to buy. When you have only the things you like and need—and they're all in good shape, not broken—it makes you feel so much lighter.

Once you've cleared out the drawers and cabinets and sorted items into piles, it's time to organize the survivors. Buy some shallow baskets, cosmetic organizing trays, or anything that would make a countertop look like it's in order. I have a beautiful ceramic, circular tray on my bathroom counter that keeps a few glass jars and ointments—all herded together so they're not spread out everywhere. Also, get some bathroom totes or plastic organizers with drawers for underneath the sink.

Stand in front of the mirror and ask yourself: *How am I going to use the items that I'm keeping?* Or, even better: *Where am I going to be standing when I use them?* We are so good at this kind of organization in the kitchen. We determine where we're going to keep our measuring cups or our pots and pans based on where we're usually standing when we need them. Why don't we do this for the bathroom? Where would it help to have your makeup when you're getting ready in the morning? Open the drawers and think about that. If you don't have enough drawer space, is there a way you can put up shelving?

For example, I keep my cotton pads, Q-tips, and facial razor (I'm Cuban and over thirty—it's a problem) all in the ceramic tray on my counter I mentioned before. These are items I use every morning and night, and sometimes in between, so I want them easily accessible. What are the items that you use most often throughout the day? You'll want to keep those in an easy-to-reach spot. You don't want to be digging through the cabinets five times a day to find the things you use a lot. The key is to just keep asking yourself: *How do I function in this room?* And organize accordingly.

Last but not least, put away all the things in your Put Away pile or basket. Anything you found in this room that doesn't belong there, put it where it belongs. Then, if you have time, wipe or vacuum out the drawers or cabinets. There seems to always be stray hairs, pieces of dental floss, or other used things in these places, and that's just gross. Do whatever you need to do to wrap up this process so you feel good about what you've done and how this room looks.

Remember, this is not a race. Even ten minutes at a time will help get you to the finish line. All that matters is a steady progress toward your goal of having a decluttered bathroom. Don't let the lie that "I'm not even going to start because it's too big a job, and I don't have time to finish" take up space in your head. Again, this all-or-nothing mentality is the thief of productivity. Just chip away a little at a time, and you'll be so encouraged by your small victories you'll find motivation to press on.

When your bathroom becomes so streamlined that you sigh a happy little sigh each time you walk into it, and you find exactly what you want and need in there—and nothing else—you are going to see and believe what a difference you can make in your entire home!

SIX

CLOSETS AND SENTIMENTAL THINGS

AH, THE CLOSETS—THE CATCHALLS OF THE HOUSE. GIRL, we are going to jump into this together, and I'm going to help you make decisions you can feel good about. So, gear up, Buttercup.

For now, we're going to focus on all the closets in your house *except* for the ones you use as wardrobes. We'll cover those later. One small chunk of progress at a time.

If you're feeling really overwhelmed, just remember that you don't have to do it all at once. It's totally okay to commit to one ten-minute portion at a time. You have enough decisions to make as it is during your day; I don't want you to spend endless hours purging only to end up with decision fatigue that keeps you from coming back to finish what we started. So take it slow and steady, focusing on short periods of time. You can always go back and do more later.

One thing to keep in mind as you move through your closets (and any other space in your home) is that it's okay to have empty space. If your house is super overstuffed right now, that can be hard to imagine. But trust me, once you get rolling, you could very well end up with less stuff than you have shelves and closets. Two of the closets in my house are nearly empty. There are lots of drawers and cabinets with nothing in them. Just because space exists doesn't mean it has to be full of stuff.

UTILITY AND STORAGE CLOSETS

There are so many different home layouts and so many different needs for this type of closet. The best way to figure out how to make this space work for you is to look at the gaps in your home. In the last home I lived in, there wasn't nearly enough pantry space. The gap we had in our home was a lack of space for the Costco-sized food we brought home for our large family.

The only closet downstairs was a utility closet located in the hallway about five feet from the kitchen pantry. Since we needed more space to fit all the food our one billion (okay, fine, four) kids eat, we decided to expand our pantry into this closet. Brian built a shelf on the wall as an extension of the pantry. It's where we kept jugs of water, cereal boxes, and other food items that wouldn't fit in the kitchen pantry. It was pantry number two. When pantry number one was out of a certain cereal, we'd go to pantry number two, pull the next box of cereal, and restock it. This solution really helped the space not feel over-cluttered. It also helped us find what we were looking for and made our home work for us, not against us, which is the point.

Since that closet was the only closet downstairs in that house, it needed to fill other gaps in our storage needs as well. Along with the shelving for food, we added hooks on the door for backpacks, purses, coats, and hats. We made it work as both a secondary pantry and a mud room.

I also noticed that since the laundry room was on the second floor, stray socks and dishcloths would end up on the floor or thrown in a pile by the stairs. Putting a small hamper in that utility closet that could be carried upstairs when I was ready to do laundry fixed this problem. Gap filled.

So how can you do this in your home? First, as always, set the intent. How do you want this part of your home to *feel*?

Next, do a visual scan. We'd been living in our house a couple of weeks when I did a scan of our lower level, and I determined what that closet needed to do for our family in order for it to be working *for* us. As you do your own scan, ask yourself these questions:

- What's littering the surfaces?
- Where are the gaps in the level of my home where this closet is located?
- What are our problem areas?
- How could I make this space work for me and my family?
- How could I turn this closet into a solution machine?

This all goes back to setting the intent in each area of your home. To set the intent for this closet (or these closets, if you have more than one), determine what the needs are in the area around the closet. **The best way to figure out how a space can work for you is to become aware of what's going on around that space currently.**

Once you've set your intent, start moving things out of that closet. I suggest you not pull everything out. Just get in there, pick up what's right in front of you, and make a decision: keep, toss, or donate. Make decisions, make piles, and get things out of that space one thing at a time. Slow, simple, steady progress gets the job done with the least amount of stress possible.

THE LINEN CLOSET

Each year during the DLAM challenge, I see women losing their minds and upending their progress by what I call the *Linen Closet Panic*. They get stuck on numbers and details that totally paralyze their progress. I receive so many messages and emails asking me to tell them exactly how many sets of sheets, blankets, and towels I have, because they want a magic number. They think if a specific number works for me, it'll work for them too.

Here's the problem with that kind of thinking: it takes away your power. My linen closet works for me, my number of kids, my climate, my preferences, and my laundry system. Your needs and wants are probably totally different from mine. For example, if you're not able to strip the beds, wash and dry those linens, and put them back on the bed the same day, you're going to need more than one set of sheets for each bed.

Decide how you want things to feel, how often you're willing to do the laundry (or are already doing it), and what will work for you. If you have a kid who wets the bed frequently, you might want to keep extra sheets. Maybe you have a child with special needs and have to change their sheets more often; if so, it's probably necessary for you to keep extras. There are a lot of things that are unique to your situation. That's why it's so important to have confidence in your knowledge of your and your family's needs. I really want to empower you to take these ideas and make them your own.

I'll offer helpful tips. I'll encourage you. I'll tell you what I do. But in the end, it's really up to you, and that's a *good* thing.

The Linen Closet Panic is always a telltale sign of a lack of confidence and that you're on your way to letting minimalism steal your joy.

This is *your* home! You know what you need. It's okay to learn from people who are good at something. But make that something your own. You don't need a set of rules. However, I totally get that seeing what other people do is a good way to discover what might work for you. So, for my family, I have:

- Two sets of sheets per bed
- Two to four spare pillowcases (because bloody

noses, boogers, and snot happen every second in my house)

- About three spare blankets for couch cuddling or added warmth
- A beach/pool towel for every person in our house (six), plus five extras for guests
- Eight bath towels for the six of us, plus two guest towels
- Two hand towels per bathroom

This is based on my family, our climate, our lifestyle, and our laundry routine. For example, I don't go weeks between loads of laundry, so it wouldn't make sense for me to have twenty-five towels. For more information about my laundry routine, visit alliecasazza.com/laundry.

When it comes to your linen closet, think about your laundry process. Not the laundry process you wish you had, or the one you're working toward, but the one you have right now in this moment. Then ask yourself how the linens in your closet can support that system.

Remember, the point of minimalism—at least the way we're doing it—is to bring you freedom. Don't let yourself get bogged down by numbers and rules. Pare down a little now and do more later if you feel it's still too much. Do whatever feels good and productive right now.

Here are a few questions to help you figure out the number of linens to keep that works for *you*:

- How many people do you have in your family?
- How often do you do laundry?
- Is it realistic for you to wash and get the sheets back on the bed in one day?
- How often do your kids get sick?
- How often do your kids wet the bed?
- Does anyone in your home have special needs that would require you to keep extra sheets or towels?
- Do you have easy access to water, such as the lake, beach, or pool?
- Do you host overnight guests often? If so, which bed do they use, and does it need extra sheets or just clean ones?

Keep in mind that if you've had a lot of towels and sheet sets for most of your life, getting intentional in this area is going to feel scary at first. It's going to feel like you're getting rid of stuff you need. But remember, the more towels you have, the more towels you will need to wash. That's more time you'll be spending on laundry. These little decisions matter because they add up. So even though paring down can feel daunting, it's important work you're doing.

Everything else in the linen closet is relative. We use loofahs instead of washcloths. If you prefer washcloths, decide how many are going to work for your family. Maybe keep it in line with how many hand towels you have.

One little rule I do have for myself is that nothing else goes in the linen closet except linens. That's the intent I set for that closet. The bath towels, the hand towels, the beach/

pool towels, the sheets, and the spare blankets are the only items I keep in there. Again, this may not work for you because you need or prefer to use the linen closet for storage as well. You do you.

When it comes to organizing the linens in this closet, it's based totally on preference. Personally, one of the main reasons I like keeping things simple is because less stuff means there is less I need to organize. I'm fine with casually folding up the sheets, sticking them in the linen closet, and walking away. But some people want the linens to be neatly folded and look really organized. Just make sure you're not turning your "need" for organization into procrastination. All you really need is to simplify.

Let's remember our goal. This way of life is not about having nothing or even about having as little as possible; it's about setting your home up to support the way you want to live. I'm set up to host friends and pool parties, take care of my kids, run my business, and live a full, amazing life. Simplicity is my tool. Let it be your tool as well.

SENTIMENTAL ITEMS

This is an area that can really trip us up because we tend to attach memories to things. Looking at an item that was once owned by someone we love or we received at a special point in our lives can take us back to a certain moment and make us feel those feelings all over again.

Sentimentality is relative. It causes us to hold on to

something because we *feel* like the item is special, not because it actually is. It's easy to attach meaning to things. The object is a visual trigger of the internal memory and the meaning you've given it.

I'm not saying to take your emotions out of decluttering. It's *good* to have possessions that are meaningful. My home decor is made up mostly of items we've collected on special trips, from special shops and special people, or in the midst of special memories. If your home is to be your haven, it makes sense that you'd want it laced with sentimental things.

However, if you keep everything that evokes a feeling in you, if everything gets marked *sentimental*, you're going to have clutter. Which means you're also going to have added stress and anxiety, the extra yucky things we're trying to get rid of.

If everything is sentimental, then nothing actually is. When you label everything (or loads and loads of things) as sentimental, what you're actually doing is removing the significance from the most precious things you own. Those items are not receiving their full value because you've given that same value to less valuable things.

Let's learn to honor sentimentality and be more conscientious of how we dish out that label. It might be helpful to replace the word *sentimental* with *unique* or *special*, because it really is easy to feel that everything is sentimental. Maybe a word change isn't what you need to make progress; maybe you just need to reframe the idea. **Letting go of objects that have memories attached to them doesn't mean you are letting go of those memories. The memories are yours forever, no matter what is stored in your home.**

I keep some special things. My old diaries and journals, a timeless red peacoat that my daughter wore when she was a baby, the first bow tie all three of my sons wore, the gloves I wore to prom the night I fell in love with my husband, and love letters from him. Those things truly are special to me. They're worth the space. But I've had other things that, even though it felt like they were special, were not really worth the time and space they took up in my home.

Letting go of the excess and making space for what matters do not mean you can't keep anything special. Minimalism shouldn't mean only keeping what you need to survive. But if you have boxes and boxes full of keepsakes, if they're piled up so high you aren't even able to enjoy looking through the memories or finding the one you're looking for, it might be time to get a little more intentional and do some paring down.

One of my favorite things is to help people find *useful ways* to keep sentimental items in their home. "Keep it" and "get rid of it" are not the only two options to choose from. Isn't that good news? The third option is "use it."

Here are some practical ways to help you honor your history and your memories without holding on to clutter.

FIND A WAY TO DISPLAY YOUR SENTIMENTAL ITEMS. What's the point of holding on to keepsakes if they're just going to be kept in a box in your closet? Your kid's kindergarten artwork, a lamp that belonged to your mom, a vase full of buttons that belonged to your grandmother—they can all be used as decor in your home. This is such a neat way to display your history, and it's a great conversation starter! Having interesting pieces like these in your home gives you a way to share your memories with other people. Plus, you'll be able to see them on a regular basis, which is so much better than storing your memories in a box in the closet.

PUT YOUR SENTIMENTAL ITEMS TO USE. Are you keeping an antique set of china dishes for a special occasion that still hasn't happened? Start using them now! Did you inherit a vintage necklace from your grandmother that you're waiting to wear to that "perfect" event sometime in the future? Why not just wear it on your next date night? Why do you hold on to things for those "special" occasions that almost never seem to happen, when you could be enjoying them now?

So go ahead. Wear the necklace, use the china, sit on the vintage sofa. I'm sure your grandma would much rather you use these things than store them and forget them. And even if not, it's yours now. It feels good to use sentimental things in the midst of normal life. What's the point in storing them and then passing them on to your kids in a box years from now, never to be used?

It's so much more special to actually use these things. And if they break, so what? It's okay. Wouldn't you rather that a piece of china break while it was being enjoyed than collect dust sitting in the back of your hallway closet? They're still just things in the end, meant to bring some happy to your space—and they served their purpose.

TAKE A PHOTO AND CAPTURE YOUR SENTIMENTAL ITEMS. Taking a photo of something special makes it easier to let it go. When my boys were younger, I found a tiny T-shirt that had been worn by all three of them but no longer fit the youngest one. It was time to pass it on to another family. I had a hard time letting it go, though, and it sat on top of my dresser for weeks. My heart would ache at the thought of donating it. Finally, I realized what I really needed was to have the memory captured. I found photos of my older two boys wearing the T-shirt, then I put it on our youngest son and took a picture of him in it one last time. It was *super* snug and looked hilarious on him, but knowing I had pictures of all three of my boys in that tiny T-shirt helped me donate it. I gave it to a friend who was expecting her first boy and seeing him wear it was the happiest thing for me!

SEND IT TO THE CLOUD. If it's a special piece of paper like a letter or a piece of artwork you want to save but not display, take a photo and upload it to the cloud or whatever form of storage system you use. This way you can still have it forever without it taking up your physical space. I've even done this with photos of non-paper items as well. For years, I had a beautiful quilt my great-grandmother knitted, but it was falling apart. I snapped a photo of it laid out on my floor and still have it in the cloud. Capturing the item before letting it go can be therapeutic. It's like you're giving the item space and honor before you release its physical form.

———

Remember, there are no rules here. If there is something extremely special to you that you want to keep but can't use in some way, then keep it. Just be careful that you don't attach memories to so many items that they bring clutter and chaos into your home. You are not your things; your things are not your memories. Your memories are within you, not within your stuff. And remember, you are allowed to go slow; it's okay to come back later and revisit what you'd like to keep and what you're ready to let go of. **You will evolve in this process.**

Whew, girl! Closets are a big undertaking. But with the tools I've shared in this chapter, I hope you'll bust open those doors with the confidence you need to start making these storage spaces work for you and your family!

As I've said earlier, you're paying for that square footage, so make sure it's worth the time you spend making those dolla, dolla bills.

SEVEN

A KITCHEN YOU CAN'T WAIT TO COOK IN (SERIOUSLY, TRUST ME!)

AH, THE KITCHEN. THEY SAY IT'S THE HEART OF THE home. But unfortunately, most people's kitchens are suffering from seriously clogged arteries.

The kitchen is a space that tends to be easily overrun with things we only hold on to because they're already there. We rarely take inventory of what we have and what we're actually using. We've got that casserole dish Aunt Linda gave us for our wedding that we sort of hate, new things we've accumulated over the years like a dozen cute mixing bowls that we pass over for our favorite two, plus a few random hand-me-downs from Grandma Sally and Mom. It's time to focus on removing the excess from this fundamental space so it can fuel your family as it's meant to. Let's do it.

You know the drill: first, set the intent. What is this room used for? Obviously, it's where food is prepared for your family. The fuel that provides the energy your family needs to live out their purpose is cooked and prepared in this room. That's no small task!

But I want you to go beyond preparing meals. The kitchen is often where people gather when you have company over (or where they *will* gather once you've decluttered like a mother and love your home enough to have friends over). This room is where a lot of conversations take place. It's important to envision how you want to use this space, so you can set the intent and declutter the way it works for you.

As I mentioned before, the thought process here needs to be around who *you* are in the kitchen. For example, I'm not passionate about cooking. It's not an area of life I get creative in. In fact, my husband does most of the cooking for our family. So when we're making a meal, we just want to get in, get the job done, and enjoy the results as much as possible. Our kitchen reflects this about us. It's very utilitarian, with basic scratch ingredients and minimal products and tools—just what we need to create simple, tasty, healthy meals for our family.

Your kitchen should be set up to work with you, not against you. So, how do you cook? Do you do a lot of baking? What kinds of tools and appliances do you have in the kitchen that you use regularly? What items do you not have that would actually make your work in the kitchen more efficient?

The biggest tip I have here is to go in there and inspect it. Walk into your kitchen today with a paper and pen and look around. Open drawers and cupboards; let the visuals trigger any back-of-mind thoughts you have every time you're in there, such as *Why do I have the measuring spoons in that drawer, so far from the mixing bowls, when I almost always use them together?* and *Why do I still have only the small Crock-Pot we received as a wedding gift, when I really should have a larger family-size for the meals I cook now?* Take notes of what you see and don't like or would prefer to try a different way.

DISHES (PLATES AND BOWLS)

Most people tend to keep spare sets of dishes in the cabinets, but typically only use one set day-to-day. I host a live online class where I walk people through the process in the kitchen, and I always ask people to share how many extra sets of dishes they have other than their regular daily set. The average answer is *four.*

Take out your spare sets or partial sets and evaluate their usefulness to you. Do you host dinner parties for which you need these extra sets? Do you tend to use paper plates when company comes over? Based on your answers to these questions, decide whether to donate the dishes or store them somewhere else away from your everyday dishes.

If you're wondering why I'm telling you to store your extra hosting dishes in a separate cabinet, ask yourself: *What's the first thing someone in my house does when they want a clean dish?*

Answer: They get a clean one from the cabinet despite the fact that there are dishes in the sink they could wash and use. If you stop keeping more than a few dishes in your main cabinet, you eliminate the possibility of having piles and piles of dishes to clean at the end of the day, and force everyone to wash and reuse the dishes. Genius, right?

When I was initially paring down everything in our house, I was so overwhelmed that I was determined to cut things down to the bone. I was in a season of my life when I really needed the bare minimum. I pared down to one of each type of dish per person (one large dinner plate, one smaller lunch plate, a bowl, a cup, and a set of silverware). This meant that after each meal, we quickly washed whatever plate or bowl we used and set it in the drying rack next to the sink ready to use at the next meal. In other words, my sink didn't fill up with stacks of stinky, dirty dishes anymore!

This ended up working so well for us. But people are always afraid to try it because it seems like it's going to create more stress—which is so not the vibe. Trust me, love. I've seen it work over and over again and have received lots of messages from people saying so once they've tried it. If you're feeling overwhelmed, I think you should consider it. Start by setting your extra dishes aside in a box in the garage for a month and just see what happens.

The point is to simplify. There are a lot of ways to go about this, but they all involve simplifying. Maybe it works better for you to have more dishes and load them in the dishwasher throughout the day and then unload them in the morning. With either method, it's literally impossible to have a pile at the end of the day. Choose what works for you.

Here are a couple of examples that might help you.

AMELIA HAS FIVE KIDS WHO ARE HOMESCHOOLED. She and her husband run a large business together, also from home. Her kids are out of the "little" stage, and her oldest two have taken the chore of cleaning the dishes off her plate completely. After dinner each night, everyone helps clean up the kitchen, and the last dishes of the day are loaded into the dishwasher. In the morning, Amelia's oldest child empties the dishwasher before starting schoolwork. For Amelia, the goal is for things to be simple, functional, and delegated. Teamwork is key. Everyone has their job, and her home is set up to support her family. Having the bare minimum number of dishes per family member is not something Amelia needs to think about. She makes sure there's not unnecessary excess in order to maintain simplicity, and that's enough.

LEANNE IS A STAY-AT-HOME MOM OF THREE KIDS UNDER THREE. Her husband works long hours six days a week, which means she is pretty much running the house and the family on her own most of the time. For Leanne, bare minimum is key to her not losing her sanity. Paring down the number of dishes to the lowest amount possible has saved her so much time and energy! She makes the girls breakfast, then spends five minutes washing the dishes and setting them in the drying rack next to the sink. When lunchtime comes around, the dishes are dry and ready to reuse. She never has more than five dishes to clean, plus a pan or two after dinner. She loads and runs the dishwasher at night, but she doesn't have enough dishes to create a massive pile to wash if she falls behind during the day. This brings her so much peace of mind and works best for her lifestyle.

———

So what's going to work best for you? Are you more like Leanne or Amelia? Something in between? Something totally different? Find a version of simplifying the dishes that will serve you and your family for the current season you're in. Just don't leave it the way it currently is if it's not working.

After you have streamlined and organized your dishes in a way that works for you, and you find there is a very special set that you love but rarely use and can't bring yourself to get rid of (e.g., Grandma's china or your basic whites for your holiday entertaining), pack them up in a box for safekeeping and place them in an easily accessible closet or shelf in the garage. You'll have peace of mind knowing they're available when you need them but stored where they won't get in the way of your everyday, functional kitchen.

SILVERWARE DRAWER AND UTENSILS

When it comes to the silverware drawer, I don't think it's necessary to be quite as minimal. Sometimes a kid accidentally throws a spoon away, and you want to have enough of them so you're not searching high and low when it's time to eat. In this case, I go by the space I have.

I have a drawer organizer that allows for a certain amount of space for spoons, a certain amount for forks, and so on. That's my limit. Also, I prefer to have things off the counters (we'll talk about that in a second), so I keep the cutlery knives in a drawer. For us it's a separate drawer from the silverware, and I bought a knife organizer from Target so they're not willy-nilly in the drawer.

Personally, I like to keep my basic utensils (mixing spoons, spatulas, etc.) in a vase or a jar on the counter by the stove. It's easy to find one that's beautiful and looks great on your countertop! I chose all wooden utensils, and they sit in a white ceramic holder. It's little touches like this that make me happy to spend time in my kitchen.

CUPS AND MUGS

Let's talk about mugs and cups. Go through your mug cabinet and quickly purge all the mugs you kind of hate. I don't know why, but we all have them. Why do we keep them? We really should only keep the coffee mugs that we search for on Monday mornings. You know, the ones that make us smile and somehow make coffee taste even better.

I know you've got a specific mug in mind right now (see?). Keep mugs like *that* one! **Life is too short to drink out of a fugly mug.**

How's your cup situation? Mismatched? I thought so. I solved my mismatched cup situation by ditching them all and buying two cases of mason jars. They all match, they look cute when they're in use, and if I need more, I can get them at any store without worrying about having mismatched sets. Win-win.

Here's a bonus tip for those of you with little kids in the house: I love the four-ounce mason jars for kids! They even have different-colored lids for this size—and straws to fit. You could get a different color for each kid in your house, so everybody knows which cup is theirs.

Or, if you're a DIY kind of girl, get a pack of the tiny mason jars, drill a hole in the lids, chalk-paint them, then stick a rubber grommet in the hole to create the perfect place for a straw. I used those for my kids and wrote their names (or a symbol like a heart or smiley when they couldn't read their names) with chalk on the lids. This worked great because the kids weren't drinking out of plastic, they knew which cup was theirs, and it kept the cups all matching.

POTS AND PANS

This is one place where setting the intent for the room and knowing who *you* are specifically when it comes to your kitchen helps tremendously.

What kinds of meals do you cook? Do you use large family-size pots, or do you tend to cook small amounts in a one-quart pan? Do you *never* use a certain type of pan that you've had since your wedding? Do you have multiple skillets but always grab the same one or two? Whatever you never use needs to go, plain and simple.

Be ruthless here—pots and pans take up a lot of space. Also, if you notice some are getting scratched up and worn out, it may be time to replace them.

APPLIANCES

First things first: ditch the doubles.

I once worked with a woman who had a KitchenAid stand mixer and two hand mixers. It wasn't like she was a major cook or professional baker or anything. She'd just accumulated a lot more than was necessary for who she was in her kitchen. She realized she never used her stand mixer. So, even though it was pretty, she chose to have visual white space and sold it. She ended up getting about $250 for it and bought herself a brand-new (and much needed) set of pots and pans with the money, replacing her old damaged set altogether. Score! She also ditched one of the old hand mixers and kept just the newer of the two.

When it comes to appliances, the main question is (again), what do *you* use? It's okay to have more than one thing if you have a reason and it's used. For example, I have two Crock-Pots and an Instant Pot because of my family size and the fact that we host a lot of parties. They each get used *all the time.* See how this works?

Appliances are usually bulky to store. So be quite critical here when considering whether or not to keep something. Do you really use this item often enough to justify the space it takes up in your life? Is there a smaller or simpler utensil that can get the job done for you? If it's something you must keep but rarely use, and your kitchen is very tight on space, consider storing it in a lower-value real estate area of your home, like a high shelf in the pantry or even a dedicated area in a spare closet.

COUNTERTOPS

This kind of ties into appliances because so many people store their appliances on top of their countertops. We're gonna shake things up, though. I want you to clear your counters as much as possible! Having visual white space in a room is an easy way to make it feel better. It makes the room feel more open, airy, and vibey. So let's make it happen.

First, ask yourself, what appliances are used so often that it would be completely pointless and unhelpful to store them anywhere but the countertop? For me, that's my coffee maker and my stand mixer. Both of those things are used literally every day, sometimes multiple times a day. So they live on my counter. Everything else—toaster oven, Crock-Pot, food processor, and so on—gets stored *underneath* the counters. I don't want to stare at a bunch of ugly machines every time I walk into my kitchen. It only takes five seconds to get an appliance out or put it away when you're done, and storing them like this provides you with so much more visual white space that impacts how people feel and work in your kitchen.

If you're worried that you might not have enough space to clear your counters, try decluttering what you're not using first and then see. If you seriously lack space, that's okay; you just have to be creative. (Most American kitchens—even small apartment kitchens—are huge by international standards!) Utilize vertical space, use the space on the side of the end cabinet, look on Pinterest for creative storage solutions and spend time making them happen. I want you to enjoy being in your kitchen, and you can—it just takes a bit of intention and creativity.

Let's talk about when your counters are a catchall for non-kitchen things, such as your keys, paperwork, mail, and more. Here's my rule: **where stuff collects, create a storage solution.**

It isn't super realistic to try to completely change your family's habits and traffic flows in the home. While habits certainly can be changed, sometimes it's wiser and easier to create a solution in an area where stuff tends to get dropped. **Create a solution that supports your habits, rather than stressing out over trying to change the way you or your family members have done things for years.**

One example of how I've done this in our home is by placing a basket at the bottom of the stairs. When we moved into this house, having two levels in our home was new for us. I quickly found that stuff collects at the bottom of the stairs because we're too lazy to take it back upstairs if we're not already going up anyway. I decided to google the problem to see what other people who live in two-story houses were doing, and all I saw were things like, "Just nip the laziness in the bud. Have a rule in your house that things get taken upstairs right away and that's that." Uh, not gonna work for me.

I'm the one who's too lazy to go up and down the stairs all day when I've got a business to run and food to prep and kids to educate. It wouldn't feel right to demand that my family take their items upstairs as soon as they're done using them when I'm not doing that myself. So I made my own solution.

I bought a rectangular basket with a lid that went with my decor and placed it against the wall at the bottom of the stairs. I declared that this is where things go when you're done using them downstairs, but their home is upstairs. At the end of the day, we do a quick family cleanup. The basket gets carried upstairs, emptied, and brought back down when everything in it is put away. Easier than breaking habits and nagging!

So, how can we utilize this idea in the kitchen if that's where stuff tends to get dropped? Maybe it's putting a bowl on the counter for keys, hooks on a wall, or a basket by the back door. Paperwork and mail, bills, papers from school—these are big deals in the kitchen. Can you address these? Maybe you need an in-box, out-box, or to-do type of vertical organizer.

If stuff tends to collect in a room, notice where and when and how, then create a simple solution in that space.

THE PANTRY

I don't have a perfectly organized pantry. The fact is, I just don't care; and this part of our house gets used a ton, so prim and perfect organization just ain't gonna fly. Let's keep this simple, shall we?

First, throw away what is expired and what is ruined. Donate what is still sealed that you know you won't eat. (Get honest with yourself about those raw almonds on the back of that shelf—maybe you're just not an almond kinda girl.) Then store stuff better so you can access what you're keeping.

I have a couple of simple bins for like items (cans, bagged snacks and chips, stocks, etc.) and that's pretty much it. It doesn't have to be perfect, but it does need to work with you rather than against you.

———

Alright, friend. Now it's in your hands.

What intent will you set for the hub of your home? How do you want to feel when you walk in there? How do you want your family to feel? Guests? What kind of space does your kitchen have? Lots? Almost none?

Who are *you* in the kitchen? Are you a Master Chef or Queen of Quick and Simple when it comes to cooking? Your kitchen should reflect *you*, how *you* use it, and what *you* need it to be.

Imagine a week from now when you walk into your kitchen after a long day. You're pretty dang tired, but you know your family still needs to be fed. How much easier will it be to muster the energy to make dinner if your kitchen is a space you love, everything is organized and where you need it to be, there's a little vase of fresh wildflowers by the sink, and the ingredients you need are simply organized in the fridge?

Maybe these little changes will inspire you to pour a glass of wine, put on some music, and get cooking. Maybe your appreciation for the ability to provide food for your family will grow. Maybe your perspective will shift. Maybe you'll end up liking this time of day more than you used to. All from a few simple tricks for one room! Who knew?

I did. ;)

EIGHT

MINIMALISM AND KIDS

BEFORE WE DIVE INTO THE *WHY* AND *HOW-TO* OF decluttering kids' things, I want to speak directly to the moms here: You are a great mom. You're doing an incredible job. Everything you've done with your kids, everything you've bought for them, has for sure come out of the highest, most loving intentions. You are amazing, you are worthy, you are the perfect mom for your kids.

Raising kids in this lifestyle of less and with more intention is something I talk about *all the time*. In this chapter, I'm going to help you take a step back, reevaluate, and free yourself—and your kids—from the overwhelming culture of materialism that is taking over our society. And it all goes back to setting the intent (because, of course it does).

Before we tackle a space in our homes, we need to ask ourselves how we want that room to feel and work for our families. But, this time, let's go a little further. I want to encourage you to set the intent for something bigger than a specific space or room. I want you to **set the intent for the childhood that's taking place in your home.**

This is sacred. It's something we often think about long before we become parents. We have goals, dreams, and aspirations of what parenthood and, in turn, our kids' childhood will look like. What often happens, though, is once we have a child, we get so busy reacting to different situations that we forget what we set out to do. After a baby is born, we're suddenly dealing with all-night crying sessions, breastfeeding problems or formula searches, teething, diapers, potty training, and on and on. We end up reacting to so much of life in such a short time that we can barely take a breath, much less stop to think about that pre-baby intention.

There's nothing inherently terrible about doing that. It's life, it's parenting, and we've all done it. It's how we learn. But just for this moment I want you to put this book down and ask yourself: *What kind of childhood do I really want for my kids? What do I want their childhood to feel like?*

I asked myself this question when my kids were really little, and I'm so glad I did. As soon as I started thinking about my answer, all of these images came into my head of them playing outside, feeling the California sunshine on their skin every day. I wanted them making mud pies and riding bikes and finding bugs to collect in little jars. I wanted them to experience nature while also knowing the joy of playing Donkey Kong and having movie nights. I wanted them to feel good and safe in our home. I wanted the toys they had to help them cultivate their imagination and creativity, not distract or overstimulate them. I wanted to encourage a sense of family togetherness and close sibling bonds.

Getting clear on our intention for our kids' childhoods really helped Brian and me to realize our core values in parenting, our core values as a family, and what we want to instill in these little people as they live out their childhoods in our home. That intention helped me decide what toys and items deserved a place in our home and what did not. Setting the intent for their childhood served as a baseline, a decision-making tool, for what to keep and what to toss.

The actions you take in this chapter are going to be based on the intent you set for your kids' childhood. That intent might look different for you than it did for me. It will look different for you than it does for your neighbor, or your sister, or the women you see at the park and at work. That's okay. This is about *you* and what *you* feel pulled to create for *your* children. You are the one who has been divinely chosen out of every woman who has ever lived to be your kids' mom. Read that last sentence again. You are a mother with a purpose. Be empowered by that truth and own it.

So, what do you want for your kids? How do you picture the rest of their childhood going? It's okay if they're not super little anymore. Start where you are. From this point on, what do you envision? How much time do you want them to spend on technology (e.g., playing video games, watching TV, listening to music, etc.)? Do you feel pretty relaxed about that, or do you really want them to spend less time using tech devices and more time outside? What climate do you live in? Is that feasible where you live? What kind of outdoor space do you have?

If you have more than one child in your house, how do you want them to interact with each other? What kind of connection do you want to help your children foster within themselves? This last question ended up being a really important goal of mine as a mom. I want to empower my kids to have self-awareness, self-confidence, and self-esteem. And, believe it or not, even that has a lot to do with what we do or don't keep in our homes. Everything is so connected.

This is the reason I want our home to feel good. This is the reason I care that it's clean, uncluttered, and not a giant source of stress. If your environment influences you, isn't it important to create one that fosters positive traits? Isn't it true that teaching our kids to value the space we live in and to take care of it also teaches them to value and care for themselves and others?

Let's open our eyes to what the environment is like around us. There's so much power in taking that action. It makes you think and act differently. It creates a higher standard for your parenting and gives your kids a higher standard to live by. It gives them confidence. If you create a clean, tidy space where they and their friends feel safe and good, they will probably want to spend time there even as they get older. This is an investment in the relationships that take place in your home.

I hear from women all the time who wish they had realized this sooner or had done better. They allow guilt to wash over them and discourage them. I don't want that for you! Listen, knowledge is power; awareness is power. So let's be grateful for the lesson and choose to be more aware moving forward. Let's be coachable women who can learn from one another. Let's allow these little perspective shifts to help us do better. What you're doing is big, mama. It will have an impact, and maybe there's a reason you didn't learn this until right now.

No matter where you are or what your life looks like, no matter what your socioeconomic status is, this can help you. It can work for you. It has nothing to do with what kind of house you live in or how much money you make. Whether you live in an eleven-bedroom mansion in Beverly Hills or a tiny house you can barely afford in the middle of what feels like Nowhere, USA, this is about you and your kids. This is about cultivating an environment for your kids in a way that feels really good to you and them.

There is purpose in your home, and you get to decide what that purpose is. You get to determine the environment your kids are going to grow up in. Again, own that power.

KID STUFF: LET'S DIVE IN

This is one of the most important tips I can give you: **If your kids are old enough to notice, don't go behind their backs and get rid of all their stuff.** Don't do it. It will end with your kids feeling like they don't have any say. It can often cause kids to feel violated, scared, worried, and like they can't trust you. Feeling out of control with your own things and space is not a good feeling for anyone, especially a child.

I know you might be thinking: *But Allie, how am I supposed to get through to them? They won't listen. They hold on to* everything. *They want everything. I have to do it this way.*

DECLUTTER LIKE A MOTHER

No, you don't. I wholeheartedly believe that we have a responsibly to raise our kids in a simplistic way and give them an understanding of the place material items should have in their lives. I believe this is how we will end the wastefulness of the overly consumeristic society we're living in. But I also believe the best way you can teach this to your children is to lead by example and include them in the process. Keep things simple. Show your kids what it looks like to remove excess, then guide them through the same process with their stuff, gently and with patience.

One thing to note is that, in my experience living this out and coaching others through it, children ages three and older can and should be fully involved in the process of decluttering their things. It will probably be a slower process with them involved, but this is incredibly important.

Please remember that kids are people too, and being a kid can be really hard. As soon as they reach a certain age, they have their own viewpoints. They have their own hopes for how the day is going to go and ideas for what they want to do on the weekend. But despite all their hopes and ideas, they have almost no control over those things. Most of the time they have to just go along with whatever the grown-ups decide. And that's fine. It's not all about them. That's a good lesson to learn early, but it can still be hard.

Springing something like minimalism on them when you've lived a consumeristic lifestyle for most, if not all, of their lives can be really challenging for them. If you go about it by barging into their rooms, getting frustrated with how much stuff they have, and putting all the responsibility of purging on them without guidance, you're not going to get the outcome you really want.

So how do you implement the minimalist lifestyle in a way your child can understand? In a way that's easier for them? You learn about your kids. You learn things about them you didn't know before. You get a deeper understanding of your kids so you can set the intent for their childhood as it relates to them.

I'm going to teach you how to take the intent that you've set and apply minimalism to it as it relates to each of your children.

EVERY KID IS UNIQUE

The truth is, each child is an individual. They're not a unit. Each of them has a distinct personality, talents, hobbies, purposes, life experiences, perspectives, and motivations. We have to approach this new way of living in a way that applies to each of them as individuals. Otherwise, it's not going to go well, and it's not going to stick. The good news is, though this feels overwhelming, I'm going to walk you through it as simply as possible.

In 2019, I spent several months developing a program called Uncluttered Kids® with Amy Tirpak. Amy's background is in family therapy; she's worked as a licensed, independent clinical social worker for years in many different settings, from schools to foster care and adoption agencies to residential treatment facilities, health clinics, and private practices. She's worked with a lot of different kids experiencing different issues, including trauma, behavioral issues, and

Autism Spectrum Disorder. Amy and I combined her expertise with my experience teaching women about minimalism and simplicity to create this incredible program. Uncluttered Kids has served thousands of families in helping them lead their kids into a simplified way of life through our gentle, respectful approach.

Amy and I developed Uncluttered Kids to really dive deeply into everything that could possibly come up as you teach your child to live in a simplistic way that supports the intent you've set for their childhood. This program started as a guide to getting kids involved in minimalism, but it ended up becoming this incredible communication tool that equips parents with what they need to do to relay the importance of simplicity to their kids and how to authentically and deeply connect with them. Uncluttered Kids turned into a parenting program that has changed thousands of lives. (For more information on the Uncluttered Kids program and to receive a reader-only discount, visit alliecasazza.com/kidscourse.)

While I think this program is amazing and every parent should have it, I want to share with you a foundational piece from it. In the program, Amy shares five different personality types of children that she developed as it relates to personality traits and what motivates them.

Knowing this information will help you communicate with your child in a way they will understand. It will also help you know how to confidently teach the concept of minimalism to your kids without pushing them away from the idea.

Here are the five types and their key characteristics:

1. Empathetic and generous
   - Very aware of how people around them are feeling
   - Takes pride in making others happy
   - Is often great at sharing their things
2. Competitive
   - Always turns activities into games, challenges, or races
   - Finds a way to make a simple task a competition
   - Compares themselves to others
3. Motivated by money and things
   - Loves material things and money
   - Always wants something new
   - Finds joy in the process of purchasing something new
4. Emotional and attached
   - Loves the things they already have
   - Seems to have an attachment to everything, regardless of value
   - Identifies everything as their favorite
   - Attributes feelings to toys
5. Motivated by quality time
   - Always wants to be by your side
   - Doesn't play independently for very long
   - Often complains that things take too long
   - Views things that need to be done as obstacles to being with you

This information is so valuable! Let it enable you to know more about your child and how to communicate with

DECLUTTER LIKE A MOTHER

them, and in turn, how to empower *them* to take action for themselves.

If your child is the empathetic and generous type, you'll want to focus on how helpful they are and how they make others feel good. As you declutter, explain to them how giving their unused toys to a child who might not have much is going to make them feel.

If your child is the competitive type, focus on their strengths. Point out how well they're doing as they help you purge and turn it into a game.

If your child is the type who is motivated by money and things, make decluttering about creating space for all the cool things that will come during the holidays or their next birthday, or give them an incentive, like if they get rid of ten unused toys, you'll give them a dollar.

If your child is the emotional and attached type, acknowledge that things are special instead of dismissing it, and verbalize when and why you need to get rid of things. The key here is to make your child feel seen and heard, and to empathize with them even if their sentiments seem silly to you.

If your child is the type motivated by quality time, make decluttering about spending time together. Invite them to sit with you and do this activity together. These kids just want to spend time with you.

So, which type is your kid? If you aren't sure, you're invited to take the free quiz Amy and I developed, which is available at alliecasazza.com/kidsquiz. Once you have this knowledge and understanding of your kids, you'll know how to empower them to make decisions and grow into little minimalists themselves.

Raising your kids in this way is seriously one of the best gifts you could give them. I'm speaking from experience.

A NOTE ABOUT SPECIAL SITUATIONS

If your child has experienced trauma, been diagnosed with a disorder or severe health issue, or is going through a big change, please know that these personality types and approaches will look a bit different as their attachment to things can manifest differently.

Kids naturally cling to things for security. Think about how common it is for a baby or toddler to have a favorite stuffed animal or blanket they take with them everywhere. When kids are small, everything can seem big and scary. There are changes happening, and they don't fully understand the big picture. They cling to that favorite object because it's a constant in their lives. To them it feels like no matter what else is happening, they at least have the assurance that their blanket or their stuffed animal is with them.

As children get a little bit older, and especially if they're dealing with a lot of insecurity in other areas, they'll become *more* attached to their toys and other objects. If there's a change happening that they don't understand, they find comfort in being able to hold on to those objects whenever they want. It gives them a sense of control: they can choose to put them in certain places in their room and when to hold them or set them down. Those are minor choices, but that sense of control helps kids feel like they have a say.

DECLUTTER LIKE A MOTHER

So, if your child has gone through or is still going through some type of difficult situation, it's okay that they're attached to their things more than other kids are. Please don't look at that as a negative symptom or something that needs correcting. It's totally normal.

Have grace and move slowly. Their little brains might be overloaded already from processing big feelings and changes, so it may take them a bit longer to embrace this new lifestyle. It's so important that they feel secure and comfortable in your home; therefore, take small steps forward and move at their pace.

HOW TO PURGE YOUR KIDS' TOYS

You've already set the intent for your kids' childhood; now it's time to carry that intention into their physical space. We can do this with their toys, clothes, bedrooms, playrooms—anything and any space that is for them. The main thing is to have a baseline (your intention) to help you (and your child if they're age three or older) make decisions. Remember, it's never too late to set the intent for your kids' childhood.

Here are some questions to help you bring the intent for their childhood to the physical spaces:

- What do you want for this space?
- What do you think your child wants for this space?
- How do you want it to feel?
- What function do you want it to have for your kids?

- What kind of childhood do you want to foster in your home? (Constantly revisit this answer!)
- Are the toys and clothes you have supporting that intent?

Do you see how setting that intent ahead of time makes it easier to decide what is worth keeping and what isn't?

Have a Plan

When you involve your kids in the decluttering process, it's helpful to have strategies in place and an attitude of excitement. Make a plan for what you're going to be doing so your kids can see that you're confident, you know what to do, and you're positive, not stressed. Kids pick up on your energy and emotions!

One super helpful tip I can give you here is to focus on what they're *keeping*, not on what they're taking away. It will help you and your kids if their attention is on choosing what their favorite things are, rather than what they're losing.

If they decide to donate a toy that is special to you but not to them, the best thing to do is to go with their decision. We want to encourage them in this process and empower them to make decisions. They're probably not going to gain confidence if they sense you're struggling with their choices. Again, kids can sense our emotions and energy, and a lot of the time, those transfer onto them. Be positive and lead by example. Relate to your child, support them, and guide them through this shift your family is making together.

What to Do with What You're Not Keeping

As always, when purging, try not to let the Donate pile sit around. We want to move that out of your space as quickly as possible!

One of the best places to donate kids' stuff is a women's shelter. I have found that these shelters exist in or near most cities, and they're always grateful for new things. The moms there are going through a very difficult time with their kids in a strange place. A lot of them have left everything behind to seek safety.

Other great places to donate include churches (for their nurseries and kids clubs), in-home day care centers (you're supporting a small business), group homes, and the Department of Social Services (getting new toys is a bright spot in many foster kids' lives).

If the toys are broken, I'm giving you permission to just throw them away. Donating broken toys just because you feel guilty about tossing them only creates more work for the donation center. They can't use them, so you're basically forcing them to throw them away for you. Also, if possible, contact these places beforehand to confirm they accept donations and which items.

A note on selling children's items: it's rarely worth the time and effort.

I don't encourage people to sell anything outside of high-value items (e.g., furniture, valuables, vintage goods, large items in good condition), and I especially advise against doing so when it comes to your kids' things.

If you want to have a yard sale, please do—and make some extra dough! Just don't let selling your things become a hang-up or time-sucker. If you decide you want to sell an item, it's helpful to have a plan and a deadline. Schedule the yard sale, buy the signs, post about it on Facebook, and make it happen. If you're selling online rather than at a yard sale, give yourself three days for the items to be taken from your house. And whatever doesn't sell gets donated. Let yourself feel good about donating things. It's not wasteful; it's generous. Deal?

Boundaries like this will prevent you from just moving clutter around instead of actually getting it out of your home.

PURGING THE TOYS

Some people feel super overwhelmed by the idea of getting rid of some of their kids' toys. They're afraid this change will make things harder for them as parents, resulting in their kids being bored and unable to play by themselves. If that's you, let's talk about it for a second.

Ralph Waldo Emerson is thought to have said, "It's a happy talent to know how to play." Children are naturals at play. They're masters of imagination. They display clearly our natural ability as humans to create ideas and entertainment.

Kids don't even need toys. In fact, many of the toys manufactured today actually hinder kids' imaginations instead of fostering them. Giving them too many toys, especially ones that discourage them from using their natural inclinations, can hold them back from their organic, playful state of being. So by taking away these toys, you are actually freeing their minds. What a gift!

I do want to emphasize that toys are not inherently bad. We have toys in our house and my kids love playing with them! But we have a limit.

In my experience, when kids have few to no toys, they learn how to create and entertain themselves, they develop longer attention spans and better social skills, they become more resourceful problem solvers, and they cultivate a love of reading, writing, art, and music. You can set up your home to be a place where imagination and creativity can run wild.

Having fewer toys also fosters gratitude. Kids tend to take better care of their things and are able to focus on what matters rather than becoming materialistic. And isn't that what we want? Isn't that the type of childhood we want our kids to have? Don't we want to raise them with these skills, abilities, and characteristics?

When my kids were little, and I hadn't figured this out yet, most of the time they would go into their playroom, dump all their toys on the floor, and walk out ten seconds later complaining that they were hungry and bored. They weren't hungry or bored; they were overstimulated by all the options in their playroom. And how could they not be? There were loads of bins with loads of toys on every wall, most of which had been tossed across the floor. Kids cannot mentally handle an overwhelming number of choices. This is backed by science.[10]

When we remove some of the choices, all of a sudden, they can cope, they can decide, they can play. The more we get out of their way, the better and longer their playtime will be.

I want to point out that changing the way you and your family have lived in relation to things is a lot, and the kids will feel this change more acutely. If you, as an adult, had lived a certain way for all or most of your life, and suddenly that way of living changed, wouldn't you need some time to adjust? Isn't it possible that you'd struggle a bit? We sometimes forget that kids are people too. Go as slowly as they need you to. Of course, so much depends on the age of the kids, the environment, the experiences they have had so far, extended family and relationships with those relatives, and more.

Some people have an in-law who is continually bringing toys for their grandkids, and it can be overwhelming. Some people don't have any support outside of their immediate family and feel totally alone. Some families are really tight on money and so are scared to get rid of things. There's so much history and so many emotions and circumstances that are at play when it comes to decluttering anything, but I find it especially difficult with children's things.

Just remember all the amazing reasons you're setting out to do this in the first place. You as the parent know what's best for your children, and this will be such a positive shift in the end. It's just that navigating through the process can be tricky. But you're an action-taker and a phenomenal mom. You've got this!

Why Organization Doesn't Work

Let's spend a moment on organization. When you organize the toys without purging, you're keeping excess stuff, and that stuff is likely going to end up dumped on the floor. Let's face it, toys do not stay organized unless Mom does it. **Organization is a temporary rearrangement, not a solution.**

The key for you in this section is to stay focused on the goal to create less clutter for you, and more of what's good for your kids. Removing the excess is the only way to get there.

How Many Toys Should You Keep?

A lot of the time, having a set number to aim for is anything but helpful. It's easy to get hung up on the numbers and miss the point. I find it's much more helpful to follow this rule: have a designated space for things like toys, and when that space fills up that is your cue to purge.

During my initial purge, I decided to have one large toy chest for all the toys. My kids were very little, and there wasn't really "Bella's toys" versus "Leland's toys"; it was just "the kids' toys." That one big toy chest worked really well for us for several years. It served as the boundary for how many toys were too much. Giving myself a limit felt so good. I felt calm and confident that the clutter wouldn't get back to where it was all too much, because now I had set a new standard. When birthdays and holidays would come and the chest got full, it was time to revisit what was inside and remove some things that weren't getting played with as often.

Once my kids were older, I decided that having a toy chest

for each child made more sense. So that's what I did. Now, each of my kids has a toy chest in their bedroom, and there's a general toy chest in the loft where they build LEGO and play together. This works great! Each kid has a place to keep the toys that are specifically theirs, and a place to put those that belong to everyone—leaving no space for arguing over "That's mine, not yours!" during our quick nighttime cleanup routine.

You can get one big toy bin for your kids to share, or you can get one for each child. You can have several smaller bins if you want. It doesn't matter. Do what feels best for you. But do set a limit on space. The toys should not take over the house, or even an entire room, without any containment. Remember, it's not good for the kids to have too many toys to choose from.

Set a space limit and let that be the new standard for how many toys you keep. Once you hit that limit, you and your kids can reevaluate the toys before any more come in. Let's be real. The toys will still end up in all parts of the house, but this standard will make it way easier to clean up and maintain. You now have one simple place to put them rather than loads of organization bins you don't have the energy to manage.

What Toys Should You Keep?

It's important not to tell your kids what is special and what is not. Let them feel. Let them decide. It's also important not to get rid of toys just because you don't think they are special. Coming from a place of control and telling your kids how to feel about their things can cause resentment to build up inside them, and that is not what we want. We want them to love this minimalist lifestyle!

Here's my suggestion for what to keep:

- toys that are truly cherished and beloved by your kids (the ones that cause meltdowns when they go missing)
- toys that encourage constructive play (think LEGO, train tracks, and puzzles)
- toys that encourage imaginative play (think art supplies, dress-up clothes, and books)
- toys that foster togetherness (think board games and family activities—even the iPad and gaming systems foster togetherness if they're playing together)

Also keep in mind that sometimes your kids will play with an ordinary toy in a way that's different from how it was originally intended, a way that's really creative. It's a good idea to keep toys like that!

For example, my mom bought my boys Mario Bros. remote-controlled race cars for Christmas one year. That's a battery-operated, pretty unimaginative type of toy. But my boys played with them constantly! They always played together (fostering togetherness), and they used them to make up stories and scenarios that the Mario Bros. would live out (fostering creativity and imagination). Those little race cars stayed long after they were given to us.

What Toys Should You Let Go?

Here are my suggestions for what to get rid of:

- random toys like those cheap, plastic ones they give you in kids' meals
- toys and games that have key pieces missing
- toys that are no longer played with, or those you *want* your kids to play with but they don't
- large toys that are not played with often enough to be worth the space they take up, such as toy kitchens

Here are some questions to ask yourself as you're purging the toys:

- Is this toy adding to my child's life in a positive way?
- Is this toy aligning with the intent I've set for their childhood? (It always goes back to this!)
- Does my child play with this toy? (A way to check this is to ask yourself if this toy is valued and searched for when it goes missing. If not, it's really just taking up space.)

I want to challenge you not to make this task of decluttering your kids' toys bigger than it is. I totally get how easy it is to overthink this. You don't want to do the "wrong" thing or harm your kids. But listen, if you allow them the time and space to be a part of this process with you, if you listen to them and follow the guidelines I gave you, it will be a good and successful experience! Also keep in mind that this doesn't need to be done all at once. If you start but then notice that your kids are really struggling, leave that area alone and move on to another area in your home. You can come back to it later.

I promise, if you lead by example, they will come around. Just start making these changes in your own life and in other parts of your home.

PURGING THE CLOTHES

Even though going through the kids' wardrobes can be overwhelming, even though clothes aren't cheap, even though they can be hard to let go of, we tend to hold on to way too much "just in case." I want to encourage you not to be afraid to make some solid decisions in this area. More clothes literally create more laundry—more work—for you. If you feel like you're constantly doing the laundry, I promise you, your kids will be fine with less clothing. You can create so much lightness in your home through this area.

A great way to start is to notice what they're actually wearing for a week or so. If you're the one dressing them each day, what outfits do you typically reach for? If they're the ones dressing themselves, what are their go-to favorites? Kids are like us. We have our favorite outfits we wear over and over, and then we have those items we keep stuffed in the back of the closet for no other reason than "just in case." We need so much less than we think we do. Pull out everything that your kids haven't worn in two weeks and ask yourself (or your kids) these questions:

- Why haven't they worn this?
- Do they like it?

- Do I like it?
- Is it stained or damaged in some way?
- Does it fit or will it fit very soon?

If they haven't worn something in a couple of weeks because it's a "special occasion" item like nice clothes for an event, family dinners, church, or something similar, that's a valid reason for holding on to it. For everything else, be real with yourself about what they actually wear and why.

You also need to think about your family's lifestyle. I don't mean the lifestyle you want to have, but the one you are actually living today. Ask yourself these questions:

- What kind of family are we?
- What do we like to do?
- Are we active?
- Do we spend a lot of time outside?
- Do we go to church?
- Do we go out to dinner often?
- Do we go to a lot of nice events?
- What kind of climate do we live in?
- Do our kids often play outside and get dirty?
- Are we homebodies?
- Do we have a good laundry system?

The answers to these questions will help you determine what kind of clothes and how many you need to keep.

Keep in mind that if you do laundry infrequently, you're going to need more clothes; otherwise, you're going to be digging through the hamper. I do a load of laundry a day, so we never run out of outfits to wear waiting for the laundry to get done, which means we don't need as many clothes.

It's important to remember what is truly wasteful as you go through this process. Don't keep something just because it feels wasteful to let it go. What is wasteful is keeping something you're not even using when someone else could use it. Let it go and move on. We've got to make some decisions and move things out of the house in order to see progress.

SPECIFIC KIDS ITEMS

I want to give a few helpful tips for things that belong to our kids but don't fit into neat toy and clothes categories. These are things that don't necessarily belong in their playrooms or bedrooms. I want to encourage you to think outside the box when it comes to these items. And remember, ease of use is key. Meaning, where and how can you store these types of things to create the easiest flow around the house as you go about your week?

Sports Equipment

If your kids are into sports, do yourself a huge favor and store their sports stuff somewhere you can easily access it but is still out of the way. Two of my boys play baseball, so there's a decent amount of equipment in our house. Storing this equipment in whoever's room it belongs to doesn't work for us because when it's time for practice, we need to be able to just grab it and go.

When the boys come home covered in dirt, they want to strip off all their gear immediately after entering. This is their habit. So I need a place for them to do this where it's not going to track dirt through the house. We made the garage their drop-off point. This way, the boys can dump their stuff and come inside clean, making it simpler for everyone. It's so much easier to create a system around your kids' habits rather than having to correct them every time they come home.

Musical Instruments

I treat this the same way I do sports equipment. We keep our son's guitar in its case, leaning against the wall, in our downstairs storage closet. It needs to be in a general living area for him to practice and easy to grab when we're heading out for lessons. Where does your kid practice? Where would it be easiest to store in your house? Pick a spot, work around their habits, and make things simple.

Art Supplies

These items can and will totally overrun your house if you let them. To keep this from happening, choose a realistic place to store them that allows for the access you want your kids to have. Maybe that's a shelf or drawer at their level where they can grab the supplies they need. Or maybe it's a higher shelf or drawer so you would need to get the items out. Choose a place you feel comfortable with and works for you and your kids, and then, based on that space, keep however many supplies will fit in that area. This is another area where it's better to decide on the space rather than focusing on a specific number you're "allowed" to keep. Remember, when they're done with an art project or run out of a certain supply, you can buy more, but only keep what will fit in that space at one time.

Artwork

Once again, if we're not intentional about this, it can get totally out of hand. Like piles and piles and hidden stacks of artwork in every room (#sendhelp).

But we also have to be careful how we take action on this issue, because we don't want to discourage passions or creativity. (Motherhood is such a damn balancing act. Every mom should get an award at the end of each week. For real.) All four of my kids draw almost every day, and my daughter, Bella, is literally always making art. So I can't keep every piece of artwork that my kids create. I have to set boundaries in order for the house to be a place that serves us, not the other way around.

It can totally make you feel guilty to sort through and get rid of your kids' creations. I'm not beyond those feelings. One way I've found to combat this hang-up is to involve my kids in the process. My kids know we can't keep everything in its physical form, so we store it digitally. There are lots of great apps you can use to take photos of the artwork and store it before tossing the physical paper. Storing art this way also makes it easy for me to print it out later if I choose. You don't need to get rid of things like this permanently; just give yourself permission to not have to keep it physically in your home.

Some of my kids' creations are just too sweet, and I want to treasure them a little longer before we move them to digital storage. For those, we keep an artwork wall in our home. This wall has changed over time and with each move. We've used tape to hang the art, and it makes for a really cute, DIY-looking gallery wall. I've also purchased frames that match our decor and created a collage wall of the kids' art. Displaying their creations makes the kids feel special and proud, and it's a great conversation starter when you have guests. This doesn't have to be an expensive venture. Go thrifting for frames, then spray-paint them all the same color to make them cohesive before hanging them on the wall.

Another option for those who want to keep a few more "originals" is to get an accordion folder. They sell them at all basic stores, and they'll give you a little more room to keep the sweetest pieces. Just remember to make decisions and avoid keeping everything.

Hand-Me-Downs

These items range from clothes to baby gear to toys. Some of you may be dealing with those from outside the family, and some are wondering what to do with sibling-to-sibling ones. I've put together some helpful tips for each of these categories.

FROM OTHERS. If you don't want the items that your sister's best friend from work generously wants to give you, you have two options:

1. Say something up front, like, "Wow, thanks so much for offering, but we don't have the space or the need

right now. Maybe someone else you know needs them more than us? Thank you though!"

2. Take them and be grateful, then donate or hand them off to someone else. You're not obligated to keep anything given to you. So if you don't want them, just say thank you and drop them off at the nearest donation center, guilt free.

If you do want the hand-me-downs, such as clothes, I encourage you to go through them first before you start putting them in the dresser or closet. See if the clothes fit (now, not in a year or two), and whether they're your style and fit your lifestyle. Just because someone gives you a bunch of J.Crew Kids clothes that are normally outside your budget doesn't mean you need them. Also, make sure they are in good condition, without stains, rips, or holes.

TIP: Sort through hand-me-downs before your kids see them. Otherwise, your child might see and fall in love with a shirt you think is hideous, or worse, one of those loud, annoying toys. (I'm looking at you, Tickle Me Elmo.) So do yourself a favor and sort through them alone.

SIBLING TO SIBLING. I absolutely pass on clothes from one kid to the next. My boys are all really close in age and size. They're literally like stairsteps; they go from one size down to the next. If something has held up long enough and it's in good condition, I keep it for the next boy, because I know he'll be able to fit into it soon if not right away. Here's my rule: if a piece of clothing will fit the next child during the next appropriate season, I still love it, and it's in good condition, I will hold on to it.

When it comes to toys, if it's something one of your kids is done playing with that a sibling really wants, pass it on. Or, if you have baby toys and are likely going to have another baby, it's totally okay to hold on to those. The point is, the keeping of these things needs to have purpose. We don't want to hold on to things "just because" or "just in case." Remember, if you hold on to everything, it's going to be too much.

Baby Gear and Baby Equipment

If you know you're planning to have another baby, and the item is a necessity or expensive, keep it but put it out of the way. You can put hooks on the walls in your garage, attic, basement, or storage closet and hang ExerSaucers, swings, and heavy gear. I had one medium-sized bin where I put the baby wrap, onesies, toys, and different things I loved, needed, or wanted to use for the next baby. Only keep things you really think you're going to use again and store them all somewhere out of the way.

Outdoor Toys

I don't really like to get rid of toys that promote imaginative or creative play, and I feel the same about toys that get my kids out in the sunshine! So I don't typically declutter them unless they're worn out. We have a large plastic bin where we store our outdoor toys—this bin is even large enough to hold scooters (plus balls, games, and the other things my kids enjoy playing with)—and we have hooks on our garage wall to hang the bikes. Keep what your kids enjoy playing with and get rid of anything that's damaged or not played with often.

———

Everything goes back to the intent that you've set for your kids' childhood. What do you want for your kids? How do you want their childhood to feel? The intent you set is going to be the biggest key in helping you decide what stays and what goes. Don't overanalyze and get bogged down by the details. Take the lessons in this chapter and apply them in a way that helps you and serves you.

NINE

A MAYBE-NOT-SO-
CAPSULE WARDROBE

THERE WAS A YEAR OF MY LIFE WHEN I TRIED HAVING A capsule wardrobe. Let me tell you, it was the *worst* idea.

Have you ever heard of a capsule wardrobe? Basically, it's a wardrobe of timeless, key pieces that you can mix, match, and layer as you need according to season. The capsule wardrobe usually only consists of a certain number of items and no more.

A few years ago, I felt self-conscious about the fact that I'm Allie Casazza, I help women simplify, I teach minimalism, yet my wardrobe wasn't capsulized. So I gave in to the trend and got rid of everything that wasn't a basic, staple piece that could be used in a very limited wardrobe. I lived this way for over a year . . . and I was absolutely miserable.

The mornings of walking into my closet excited to piece something together to express how I was feeling that day were gone. My options were gone. I felt limited because I had subscribed to a limiting closet out of obligation.

Even when I was a kid, I would spend at least an hour a week planning what I would wear to school. I even had a special notebook I would sit with in my closet and sketch out which outfit I planned to wear each day, complete with a sketched-out hairstyle inspired by the Olsen twins. (Guys, I was super cool.) Putting myself together had always been a creative outlet for me. It made me happy, and it still does.

This is who I am, who I've always been. The point is this: you have to make minimalism relative to *who you are*. You can do the same with any area of your home. When it comes to your wardrobe, maybe you'll end up with a capsule or maybe you won't. All that matters is that the way you have things set up is supporting you.

Sometimes a capsule wardrobe is a great idea. A lot of people find it very freeing because they don't have to think, and it cuts down on the time and mental energy they spend on what they're going to wear each morning. Especially if you are a busy mom who doesn't care much about putting outfits together, a capsule wardrobe could become your BFF. It could be a way you practice intentionality.

My point is that everyone is different. If putting outfits together in the morning isn't what lights you up, then keep things simple. There's nothing wrong with that. But if you're like me, and you love putting your outfits together and getting dressed is one of your favorite parts of the day, there's nothing wrong with that either. Remember, don't be a minimalist for the sake of being a minimalist. Be a minimalist only where it serves you. It should be making your life *better*. If a capsule wardrobe isn't going to do that for you, then find your own version of simplicity in this area.

Even though I love clothes, have a full closet, and enjoy shopping, I don't needlessly shop. I'm not limiting myself via someone else's rules, but there's still intentionality. When I shop, I ask myself things like, *Do I already own something similar to this? What would I wear this with? When would I wear something like this?* These questions serve as a check-in that prevents me from just buying something for the sake of buying it. **Everything needs to have a purpose when it enters my home.**

YOU DESERVE TO LOVE EVERY SINGLE THING YOU OWN

Did you read that? Every. Single. Thing. I'm going to help you figure this out, but I need you to remember this: you *deserve* to love all the things in your closet.

Every single thing I own supports *my* specific body, makes me feel amazing, and helps me live out my purpose. That may sound a bit dramatic, but it's true! The things I own help me feel ready to show up as a mom, a leader, a business owner, a human being. Your closet should be doing this for you too.

I see my clothes as an investment in me. My underwear is a perfect example of this. Let me tell you about C-sections and underwear problems. Yes, we're going there.

I've had four C-sections, and my C-section lump is real, girl. Actually, it's not so much a lump as it is a dent-and-fold. Let me tell you, there is nothing worse than going to the store, grabbing those five for $25 panties, getting home, and in the first five seconds of putting them on have the top band of the underwear roll down into your dent-and-fold. It is one of the most humbling experiences in life. That kind of underwear is the opposite of #babessupportbabes. Thanks, but no.

I love my body, and I accept myself. I hope you do too. But when mama goes to put on jeans over underwear like that, you can tell. Let me be the honest girlfriend who will get real with you and tell you that, yes, you can tell. Not only can you now visibly see the dent-and-fold, but you carry yourself differently when you're wearing underwear you don't feel sexy in. You act differently. It affects you!

Enter Spanx underwear. They have so many options, but my favorite one is the Undie-tectable® thong. It has the magical "Spanx technology" band around the tummy area. It comes up to your belly button and just smooths you out. Girl, this advice is worth buying this whole book for.

Listen, I love my body, and I'm proud of what it's accomplished. It gave me my babies. And *because of that*, I want to feel smooth and held together. I respect myself, and doing what causes me to feel great is an act of respect. I want to feel confident and comfortable. It's not comfortable to have the band stabbing you in your C-section scar. That's why I say no all day long to those flimsy undies, and yes to my always-there-making-me-look-good Spanx.

Now, I'll be up front with you. Spanx products aren't cheap. But I deserve more than that. I deserve to not settle for what's not going to support me. If it came down to a choice, I would rather make a cut somewhere else in my budget, like doing my own manicure at home instead of going to the salon or making coffee at home instead of hitting the drive-through for a latte. I'd rather invest in supportive clothing that's going to make all the difference in the way I carry myself and show up in my life.

So how can you take this feeling of worthiness and apply it to your entire wardrobe? Is your bra the right size? Is it supporting you? Do you have the colors you need? Do you have the strap styles you need for how you like to dress in each season? Do your sweatpants flatter you? Is your denim doing you favors or a disservice?

Right now, I'm wearing a pair of high-waisted sweatpants and a crop top T-shirt. I'm working from the couch today, so comfy is the goal. But I could totally throw on my tennis shoes and go run an errand or see someone I know and feel great. Feeling good and looking good are not mutually exclusive. Everything you own should be something you love. Something that works for you. Something that makes you feel better than you did before you put it on.

It makes me so sad when I hear women say things like, "Oh, I wish I could pull off a bright lipstick." Or, "I hate shopping for myself. It's so depressing!" Girl, you are bold, beautiful, and amazing. You *can* pull off that bright lip color. There is *nothing* depressing about dressing that beautiful body of yours!

No matter what shape your body is in at the moment, you are beautiful. It's time to live like it. I've had four kids, one of whom was eleven pounds (that's not a typo!). So, for me, that pretty much destroyed everything that's ever been smooth. I accept it. And you know what? **My body is perfect for**

my purpose, it does amazing things, and part of loving it back is dressing it well.

Now, there is a difference between not feeling good in your clothes because you need to prioritize your joy more, and not feeling good in anything you wear because you need to prioritize your health more. Nothing is going to make you feel good if you don't feel good. If you need to get healthy, please find a way to make the positive changes you need to get there and expand your happiness and confidence! You are so worth it!

So let's dive in. I want you to go into your closet, open your dresser drawers, look at what you have, and make some decisions. If every single thing you have doesn't make you feel the way you want to feel, I want you to ask yourself why you're treating yourself that way. Why are you settling? Is it because you don't value yourself enough? Do you feel any shame or hatred toward your body? Are you overwhelmed and don't know where to buy things or where to shop for things that make you feel better? There's always an underlying reason for why we keep what doesn't feel good. The decluttering process is far more spiritual than most people realize. (If you need someone to guide you through this inner work of purging your closet, visit alliecasazza.com/closetmindset.)

As you go through your clothes, ask yourself the following questions.

Question 1: Do I Feel Absolutely Amazing in This?

This question applies to everything. Yes, even your pajamas. If you don't feel absolutely amazing in something, what's the point of owning it?

If guilt comes up over the money you spent on something, remember that *it's not serving you and that's its job.* There's a lesson to be learned about valuing yourself enough to not buy things that don't help you feel amazing. Now you know, so you can shop smarter moving forward. Learn the lesson, be grateful for it, and let that item go.

If you feel guilty about tossing an item someone gave you, remember that we never want to keep something out of obligation. That sweater your aunt gave you for Christmas last year that makes you feel frumpy? Get rid of it. Just because someone gave you something, that doesn't mean you owe it to them to keep it in your closet when you don't even like it.

What takes up your space takes up your time. If you can't say you feel absolutely amazing in something that is taking up your closet space, it needs to go.

Question 2: When Was the Last Time I Wore This, and How Did I Feel?

By trying to remember the last time you wore each piece of clothing, what you're really doing is gaining a realistic perspective. Don't ask yourself *if* you wear it or *if you will* wear it, because it's easy to lie to yourself and step pretty far out of the zone of reality this way. Rather, ask yourself to remember the last time you wore something. This forces you to come up with some amount of time, or at least a general idea.

Maybe your answer is straightforward and definitive: you wear those jogger pants all the time, but they make you feel frumpy and encourage negative body talk in your head. Toss them! Or maybe your answer is more general: you don't remember exactly when, but the last time you wore that red dress was to some event and you felt sexy, and it still fits. Keep it! Maybe you can't remember wearing an item of clothing at all. It's probably not worth keeping then. Do you see how the question helps put things in perspective?

If you can't remember the last time you wore something, but you genuinely love it and know you'll need it if the occasion arises, that's okay. I have clothes like that myself. These are items I don't wear all the time, but when the time comes, I need it to be ready. For example, that navy blazer is not the vibe I need when I'm at home being a mom of four. But it is when I'm onstage at a working women's conference. You don't have to only keep items you wear all the time. Just make sure that the items you do keep are items you have a need for and feel great in.

If you don't love something in your closet, value yourself enough to let it go.

Question 3: Is This Damaged at All?

Again, this question is all about getting real with yourself. Don't hold on to something that has an unremovable stain just because you love it and you're bummed it got ruined. It happens. You're way too amazing to sport a stained sweater.

If something is damaged but it's repairable—like a rip or a missing button—then you need to get real with yourself. Are you going to have it fixed or fix it yourself? What's the plan of action?

If your plan is to repair it yourself, add a sewing kit and buttons (or whatever you need) to your shopping list, then get your phone out and set an alarm for one week from now. If your plan is to have it repaired, look up a tailor that is close to you and call to see what their hours and prices are. Then put those items in your car with a reminder to drop them off next time you're out.

Whatever you're planning, do something right then and there that will make you more likely to take action. When that alarm goes off and you haven't repaired the item yourself or dropped it off at the tailor's, get rid of it. Setting boundaries for yourself keeps you from getting stuck. You don't want to end up with a bag of damaged clothes sitting in the back of your closet for months or years!

"What should I do with my prepregnancy-sized clothes? And what about maternity and postpartum clothes that I may need again?"

When dealing with prepregnancy clothes after having a baby, we want to get super real with ourselves. Did you have a baby a few months ago, and you're now on a nutrition plan and actively on your way to your pre-baby body? Or has it been three years since your last baby, and you're a different size than you were before, and you're not actively doing anything to go back to your pre-baby size and you're good with this?

You don't want to hold on to things just because they once served you well. And I'm thinking the psychological effects of walking into your closet and seeing a dress that's three sizes smaller than what you wear now is probably not doing you a lot of good. Your body has given you so much. How can you honor it where it is today through the clothes that are hanging in your closet? If it doesn't fit you now and you're not actively doing something so that it will fit you in the near future, let it go.

When it comes to maternity and postpartum wear, if you're done having kids, let it go. Those pieces supported you during a season of your life you've now moved on from. But if you think you may return to that season of life, it's okay to hold on to things that would bring you support when you get there.

Remember how worthy and beautiful you are. I want you to invest in pieces that make you feel more like yourself— more beautiful. I want everything you own to support you and your body where you are.

THE HANGER TRICK

There's a little trick people who hang their clothes can use to find out what they truly do wear on a regular basis.

For one month, every time you wear an item of clothing, hang it back in your closet with the hanger facing the opposite way of the others. After the month is over, all the items hanging on a reverse hanger are things you wore—and likely wear the most.

Studies show most people wear 20 percent of their

wardrobe 80 percent of the time.[11] This is a great way to find what makes up your 20 percent.

WHAT TO DO IF YOU DECLUTTER YOUR CLOSET AND END UP WITH NEXT TO NOTHING

This chapter might have you not liking me so much. Especially if I'm pulling off blinders you've had on for a good long while. Maybe you've been telling yourself you're just a mom, so you don't need nice clothes. Or you only wear work clothes, so it doesn't matter what your personal clothes look like. Or maybe you've been telling yourself you just don't have the budget to get better things. If you've had these stories in your head and now realize you haven't been valuing yourself, and your wardrobe isn't supporting you, it can lead to an urge to throw everything in your closet into the flames. But then you'd have nothing to wear.

Even if you're not someone who loves putting outfits together, you still have to wear clothes. Unless you live in a nudist colony (you do you, boo), you wear clothes every day. So what happens when you purge your closet and end up with next to nothing but don't have the budget to replace everything?

I've been there. When I first cleaned out my wardrobe, I felt discouraged because I ended up with basically nothing, and I knew I couldn't afford to replace those items anytime soon. It was hard. But I stayed committed, because I knew I deserved to love my clothes and feel good in my life, no matter what my budget was. I figured it was better to have a tiny wardrobe I could mix and match, than to have a big wardrobe that didn't make me feel beautiful.

Since I had a *very* limited budget at the time (I'm talking zero wiggle room), I found ways to make an extra $20 to $40 by selling something I was decluttering or by saving money on groceries. I'd set my mind on one item I needed and invest in it as soon as I could—one piece at a time. Very slowly, I built a wardrobe I loved and that made me feel amazing.

Money doesn't have to be flowing for you to love your clothes. You can get creative. Look for sales, cut out something for a couple of months while you build up a few pieces, or learn how to mix and match outfits you already have. This is the age of Pinterest. Ideas are everywhere! This is totally doable if you change your perspective and stay positive about it.

REPLACING YOUR WARDROBE

When you're building your new wardrobe, ask yourself what is important to you. Do you want the clothes to be fair trade? Do you want them to be really good quality? Do you want the cost to be low? What is your most important priority when it comes to shopping brands?

When you're ready to go shopping, make sure you remember this is not a free-for-all, buy-everything-you-like kind of thing. If you're more the type who dreads shopping, don't be overwhelmed. Look online for brands and check out the ratings. Google things like "best denim for pear-shaped women" or "how to dress for wide shoulders." Do your research. Search what bloggers and influencers are saying, especially in non-sponsored posts. Read the reviews on clothing and look for reviewers who seem to have a similar body type to you.

For me, finding denim shorts that fit me right has been a lifelong struggle. Last summer, I did some research. I googled things like "best denim shorts for big thighs" and "best boyfriend shorts for big butt." I explored and bought and returned shorts until I finally found the perfect pair of boyfriend-style, high-waisted jean shorts that made my booty sing a J.Lo song. You may have to try and try again. But it's worth it! Hang in there.

In my experience, there are two easy ways to shop:

1. Plan a day without the kids and go to the mall or shopping center of your choice. Be prepared to try things on and make it an intentional time carved out for yourself. Don't forget to do online research before you go!
2. Order things online, try them on, and return what doesn't work. When I do this, I keep my returns in a basket by the front door, so I can go to UPS once a week rather than taking individual items as I decide not to keep them.

Another option, if you want to skip the research and just really hate shopping, is to try Stitch Fix. They do the shopping for you after you answer a few questions, then send you things to try on. You can send back anything you don't like and will only be charged for what you keep.

HOW TO STORE THE CLOTHES YOU'RE KEEPING

If you don't have a good system for your clothes, you need one. Let's consider how you typically do things and organize the space you have in your house for storing clothes.

If you are someone who has been storing your clothes in another part of your house (e.g., the downstairs guest closet, the coat closet, the spare room), I would encourage you to bring them to your bedroom. There's something about making your bedroom a space that's for you to rest and recharge—as well as to get ready to show up for your day—that serves as a way to honor yourself. Obviously, this doesn't apply to you if this setup is literally your only option because of the way your home is laid out. But if it's due to clutter, give yourself your closet back. Move whatever's taking up space in there and let it be your space.

Okay, back to business. Ask yourself some questions to make your space work for you. Do you usually keep everything in your dresser drawers, but then everything's wrinkled when you pull it out? Maybe you should try folding things differently. Or maybe you should just hang everything. If you have the closet space, why not? There are so many tutorials online for folding clothes. Look on Pinterest or YouTube and see if you can find a way that works for you and your clothes. Get creative and find a system that serves you.

Look at the kind of space you have and go from there. For me, I have hanging closet space as well as built-in drawers. I hang almost everything, but my athletic and loungewear get rolled and stacked in the drawers along with my underwear, socks, bras, and shapewear. In the past, I've hung only nice blouses and dresses while everything else got folded in a dresser.

Remember not to overthink or overcomplicate. What would be the *easiest* option for the space you currently have? Make decisions and take action. There are tons of great storage ideas out there, but ultimately you need to do what works best for you and your space.

TEN

HOW TO HANDLE EVERYTHING ELSE

SO FAR IN THIS BOOK, WE'VE FOCUSED HEAVILY ON THE SPACES that every house has, where clutter tends to physically manifest the most. However, I know there are other spaces you may need help with, so we'll dive into those here. I'm talking about the more general spaces in your home as well as any specific areas not every house has (e.g., office, homeschool area, craft room, etc.).

The good news is, you've already come so far and learned so much that you probably already know how to tackle these remaining spaces. Much of what we've purged together was the hard part. It gave you a foundation—a method to keep going—that will make other spaces much easier to work through, even if they are cluttered.

LIVING ROOM AND FAMILY ROOM

Time to ask the golden question: What's the intent in this space? Go stand in the room you're working on and ask yourself how you want that room to feel. How do you want it to serve your family? What's its purpose?

Sometimes when we do this, we realize the original intent of the space isn't actually what our family needs it to be. So a living room becomes a homeschool room, or a dining room becomes Mom's office. What do *you* need from this space in your home? Decide. Get super clear. And make decisions from that clarity.

Let me use my own home as an example. We have both a living room and a family room. In the family room, my intent was to encourage togetherness. This is a space where the kids hang out and watch a movie, the boys and I play Super Nintendo, Brian and I snuggle and watch *The Office*. This is where friends gather with plenty of room to sit. This intent helped me decide what will go in this room and what won't. I don't keep anything but the sofas, the bookcase, the TV, and cozy throws in this space. There is no storage for stuff because stuff does not belong here. The sofas are from IKEA; there's nothing expensive the kids can't roughhouse around. This is a space for regular life, for people to relax and put their feet up.

In my living room, my intent was to create a beautiful space where I could sit in the mornings and read while having coffee or sit with a girlfriend and talk while the kids play in the family room. The furniture, the decor, the entire space echoes this intent. This is not the space for the kids to eat a snack and play.

Having distinctly different spaces in your home will serve your family well. It will help everyone understand what the expectations are and what the purpose is for each space. Our home feels cozy and especially designed for the way we are together. It wouldn't feel this way if the toys were in every room or the TV was in the room with the formal couch.

Your space can be both beautiful and functional. They're not mutually exclusive! Put a toy chest that matches your style in the family room, so your toddler has toys in the general area to play with, not just in his room. Put a pretty basket in the corner to hold cozy throws. Layer rugs on the floor to make a modern room more inviting. Bring in plants and white paint to wake a space up and make it brighter. (If visual examples inspire you, take a look at my living room and family room by going to alliecasazza.com/myhouse.)

Ask the question: What would be in this space if it was exactly what my family needs it to be for the way we live?

THE CLUTTER CRUTCH

Remember the clutter crutch from chapter 4? When we first started, I told you to leave this dreaded space for later, and here we are. Your time has come, my young apprentice.

This is no small thing. I've literally seen a grown man cry while purging what was shoved in the clutter crutch. Stuff has all kinds of meaning attached to it and that's okay. But don't worry; I got you. You are ready for this.

Tackling the clutter crutch can feel so daunting that you just want to keep avoiding it. But let me tell you from experience how *good* it feels when it's done. You will *finally* have this stressful space (or spaces) clear of clutter.

My clutter crutch back in the day was the main bed-room. So every time I started or ended a busy day, I would be reminded of every unmade decision and stressful pile of junk in my house. That's the opposite of the restful haven your bedroom is supposed to be.

Remember also the effect out-of-sight clutter has on the mind. It's a lot and it matters. We want to clear as much physical space as possible, because it will end up cluttering your mental space as well.

The clutter crutch can be almost any space in your home: a guest room, an office space, a bedroom, a closet, a cabinet, even a piece of furniture can be used to store clutter. The clutter in a clutter crutch is always a physical manifestation of unmade decisions. Sentimental items you haven't decided what to do with, old toys and clothes you know you need to go through but haven't, paperwork that needs to be scanned and shredded or processed, CDs and DVDs that need to be digitized, halfway finished projects you know you won't complete but feel bad getting rid of—things like these make this space a sort of Decision Purgatory.

When you're ready to take on the clutter crutch, the main thing to remember is that you're going in to make decisions. Begin with the intention of finally clearing this space—to boldly make decisions and move things out.

Here are a few practical tips to help you knock this out.

1. JUST DO IT. I know that's annoying advice you've probably heard many times, but seriously—stop overthinking it and just dive in. The way you eat an elephant is to take one bite

at a time. Gross, but accurate. Just start with one thing. Pick it up and make a decision about it. Spend one day knocking this space out once and for all, so you'll never have to go back to it. This is the fastest, least stressful, most rip-the-Band-Aid-off approach.

2. BREAK IT UP INTO A COUPLE OF SCHEDULED DAYS. Look at your calendar and block out chunks of time over two to three days for tackling the clutter crutch. Maybe it's two hours tomorrow and four hours on Saturday. Whenever it is, block it out, commit to it, and make it happen.

3. MAKE IT FUN. Call a friend over and offer to buy pizza and beer. Play Taylor Swift as loudly as humanly possible while you dance through the decisions. Involve your spouse and kids (or don't if that's not fun). Sometimes, bringing in a fun, supportive person or playlist is all you need to finally ditch this stressor.

4. DO IT THE DLAM WAY AND SET A TIMER. There's a productivity hack called the Pomodoro Technique. Basically, you set a timer for twenty-five minutes and bust through work the entire time. When the timer goes off, you take a five-minute break. Then you go back to another twenty-five-minute jam session. You keep going until you're done. Get the picture? Small chunks of massive progress make it feel less daunting and get the job done. The annual DLAM challenge is based on the idea of small chunks of big progress. Handling the clutter crutch this way as well is totally fine!

Go, girl. Just get it done. You've done way harder things than this! You've got this.

THE GARAGE

The garage is a common clutter crutch. So if that's the case for you, read the above section and deal with this space accordingly, then come back here.

The garage is a space in your home that could support your family and work for you. I think sometimes we forget that and treat it like an extra-large closet where we dump random stuff and things we don't want to keep inside the house. What if we made it functional and helpful? What if we didn't dread going in there? What if it wasn't embarrassing to have the door open for the neighbors to see? Let's get our garage functional.

My favorite thing about our garage is the wall storage. We hook our bikes and helmets, beach chairs, gardening tools, and kids' scooters on that wall. The opposite wall has large metal shelves and drawers attached to them for Brian's things: outdoor gear, fishing supplies, workout shoes, and hand weights. There's a wall cabinet for tools, paint, and household maintenance supplies like light bulbs and air filters. There are roof racks where we store seasonal items like our large cooler and things we use sometimes but don't need easy access to. Also, utilizing the wall space this way frees up the floor space. We have so much empty floor space in the garage that we were able to turn it into a gym and cancel our memberships.

Our garage is not a storage space for everything we've ever owned but don't want in the house; it's a space that supports us and provides space for what we need. It's square footage well used.

I've even seen people in my Facebook group clear their garages out and turn them into play spaces for the kids, complete with a climbing wall and slide. In our old house, the garage was my office. How do you need this space to work for you? How can you get smarter about the way you store things? Maybe your goal is just to have enough space to park your car and walk inside without tripping over the kids' bikes and yelling an expletive. This is a good goal.

Brian and I know a couple who wanted to park their new car in their garage after a hailstorm totaled their previous car, but their garage was stacked floor to ceiling with empty boxes they were saving for a possible future business. Sorting through the boxes felt incredibly overwhelming for the woman. She was so afraid to let them go in case she needed them one day and was overwhelmed by the task of cutting them down and throwing them out. Brian encouraged her to just start with one box and do what she could. Two weeks later she told us the boxes were all gone, and they were able to park their car in their garage just before a second storm hit.

Go into your garage and pick a corner to start from. Clear that one part, make decisions, and get rid of what you don't need and use. After you've purged, look around at what's left.

What are the types of things you use your garage to store? How can you store those items in a way that leaves you the most space? How can you utilize vertical wall space? Do you need to buy a few bins, hooks, or shelves? What is the intent you set for this space? How does it need to work for you and your family?

Think outside the box and get creative until it's functional.

OFFICE SPACE

The space where I work is sacred. My intention for this place in my home is so important to me. It's a space where I provide for my family, where I create content that I hope will change the world, and where money and ideas freely flow. This space supports me as I support the women of the world, my family, and my team. It's got a big job to do because I have a big job to do, and I don't take that lightly.

When I was designing my home office, this intention made every decision for me. The room is white and light and happy. Everything in this space was deliberately chosen to align with the intent I set for it. I also wanted the energy of abundance in this space, so I purchased decor exclusively from small, women-owned shops. It made me feel like this is a space that supports small businesses as I am running mine, and I am reminded of this every time I'm in here. My office is so inspiring for me.

Your intent for this space (and any space) needs to have a practical side to it too. For example, I record a lot of videos in my office, so I intentionally styled the background to provide a backdrop that is beautiful and feels very "me."

How can you infuse your workspace with this same energy? Even if you work at the kitchen table or a small desk in the corner of your living room, this can be done with a little bit of intention. So often we buy things just because we need to fill the space, need something functional, or it's on sale, and we miss out on an opportunity to really make our space come alive and bring us joy.

What's your intent for your workspace? What do you need it to do for you? How do you want to feel in here? How can you bring the energy you need to accomplish everything you do into this space through furniture, decor, and layout?

HOBBY SPACES

Some people have a room in their home dedicated to a hobby or activity, like a craft room, sewing room, or a garage-turned-woodshop. The thing about spaces like this is that they can *feel* excessive or cluttered, but that's not always true.

Is this an activity you still actively participate in? Then the room has a purpose. Is it something you love doing and wish you had more time for? Then the room still has a purpose.

The thing we want to watch out for is whether this space has become so overstuffed that it's no longer functional, or you avoid being in there because it's so messy. If this is the case, the room is not serving its purpose. Go back to the methodology in this book and remove the excess. Make decisions. What needs to happen for this space to serve you well? What needs to change for you to get back to loving this activity like you once did? You're creating more time for what matters to you by decluttering it.

It's perfectly okay to have hobby spaces in your home if it is supporting how you live, not how you wish you lived. What I mean by this is that sometimes you have an ideal version of yourself in your head, a version that lives outside of your reality and does things you don't actually do anymore.

It is how you *wish* you were living, not how you really are. It's often based on your past. And breaking up with a past version of yourself is hard to do. Admitting you are no longer a person who sews when that used to be a part of your identity can feel gut-wrenching.

You just need to make some decisions here. (Do you see how clutter always goes back to unmade decisions?) Are you ready to move on from this chapter of your life, or are you going to commit to making time for this activity in your current reality?

It's okay to evolve. It's okay to change. That's what humans do, especially humans who become mothers and have had their priorities shift. What's going to feel good and what's doable here? Is it letting go of the past and moving into the new version of who you are? Or is it revisiting this activity and deliberately making space in your life to enjoy it?

Make decisions and create a space that is serving you as you are today.

Q&A

I'm here to help you, so I want to answer a few questions I see all the time. If you have a situation or problem that is not addressed in this book and wish you could get help with it, join the Facebook community and ask! The women there are so positive and helpful. My team and I hang out there too, so come find us at alliecasazza.com/community.

How do I get my husband/partner
on board with all of this?

Every relationship is different, and the way each couple communicates is unique to them. However, if you believe this is going to be a game changer for you as a mom, and in turn, for your family, you have every right to want to make these changes and communicate that to the person you're doing life with. There are ways to talk about these shifts without coming off as controlling or threatening to your partner's boundaries. Explain your heart behind it, share your *why*, and set your own boundaries. If things getting lighter for you are a nonnegotiable, you can respectfully say so while remembering that not everyone in your house is going to be on the same page right away.

I have boxes full of photos. How can
I digitize them? And how do I decide
which ones to keep a hard copy of?

First you need a way to scan your photos. You want these to stay in the best possible quality, so I would recommend purchasing an actual scanner. (For my scanner recommendations, visit alliecasazza.com/recs.) If you prefer to use an app, I suggest Google PhotoScan. When choosing which photos to keep a physical copy of, decide which ones are frameable—those that are your absolute favorite, you want to see every day, and are worth purchasing a frame for and actually hanging on the wall. If you have lots and lots of photos to sort through, make it an event. Maybe it can be your Monday night thing for a while. Pour some wine or brew some tea, get cozy, turn on your favorite TV show or music, and just start sorting. Put this to-do on your calendar every week until you're done.

What papers do I need to keep and what's okay to get rid of or move to the cloud?

Always keep documents you need the physical copies of (e.g., marriage certificate, birth certificates, social security cards, tax returns, business licenses, etc.). It's a good idea to keep your tax returns for seven years after filing. This sort of paperwork doesn't take up much space, so having a small filing cabinet in a closet works great and is uncomplicated. Everything else can be digitized. For paperwork that comes from the kids' school, I take a picture with my phone and store it in a folder within the photos app called School Papers. I do the same with any important papers I may need to reference but don't need the hard copy of.

Do you have tips for the dreaded kitchen countertop catchall spot where everyone dumps their stuff?

Remember the tip I gave before? Where stuff collects, create a solution. If there's a spot in your house where your family tends to drop their things—not clutter but things they use and need—create a storage solution in that location. Sometimes it's as easy as getting a key dish for the counter or hooks for coats by the front door. Other times you may need to get more creative. Pinterest is a great tool to get ideas for your particular space. I like to walk through my house when things feel like they're not working and locate the specific problem areas. I notice what types of things are accumulating in each area and think about possible solutions.

I'm worried I'll get rid of something, then end up needing it one day. It's holding me back, but I feel it's a legitimate worry. What do I do?

If there's a legitimate scenario you're waiting to play out before getting rid of something, that's okay. For example, if you're in the process of adopting a child, but you don't know what gender they'll be, and so you're holding on to a few items that can be used if the child is a girl, that makes sense. You can get rid of what is not needed once that situation works itself out. However, if you're holding on to lots of different items because you're worried you'll need them later, what you're really doing is giving in to fear and letting it make decisions for you. We do not want to be making decisions out of fear! Remember, what takes up your space takes up your time. This is your life we're talking about here. Is it worth it? Give yourself permission to rebuy that extra spatula if you truly need it down the road. If you haven't used it in months, and it's something you could rebuy in less than twenty minutes for less than $20, let it go. This is so much better than making fear-based decisions or holding on to too much for a situation that likely will never happen.

ELEVEN

MAINTENANCE MODE

GIRL, MAKE A MARGARITA OR ORDER TACOS OR BOTH.
You finished all the main rooms in your house! Ahhh! I am
so proud of you!

Let's talk about what happens now—after the celebration.
What happens after all your rooms have been purged and
your home feels lighter? You enter maintenance mode.

Decluttering is not a one-and-done kind of thing. But
it's okay, because if you can get a grasp on maintaining what
you did, you won't have to go back to the way things were.
Like any other lifestyle change, minimalism is something
you live out for good, not something you do once and then
walk away from.

You don't one day decide you want to be a healthier person,
and then suddenly just know everything you need to know
about getting healthy. You aren't able to magically implement
all the necessary changes flawlessly and immediately—even
after reading a book. Changing your lifestyle is always a

process. You learn lessons over time, and sometimes again and again.

What you chose to get rid of when you worked through your space the first time was good. But in a few weeks, you may find that you could get rid of even more. That's because you evolve in this lifestyle as you go. As your confidence in your decision making and in the minimalist lifestyle grows, you may realize you don't need as much as you thought you did. You may want to do another round of purging. You may find yourself releasing items into the donation bin as you clean up at the end of each night. This is good! It's all part of the process.

How do you know when you're finished with your initial purge? *You* decide. There is no list of standards to meet or number of things to put in the trash. You get to decide what's good enough for you right now. You focus on progress, not perfection; you focus on what you think is going to work for you and your family, not on what works for someone else. When you've moved through all your spaces this way, you're done! Or at least your first round is done, and you enter maintenance mode.

For me and my family, maintenance mode looks pretty simple. We live a different way than most families, which means we're always questioning what comes into our space. As we do our nightly cleanup and find something random that falls under the "clutter" category, it goes in the trash or the donation bin we keep in the back of the car.

Keeping an eye out during day-to-day cleanup helps, but the key to keeping these random things at bay is regular maintenance purges. You can do these once a week, once a month, once a quarter, whenever you want. Many of my Your

Uncluttered Home students find it helpful to do maintenance purges more often in the beginning, fresh out of their initial purge. Then they move into seasonal purges, which is what we do in my house. The change of the seasons acts as a mental trigger—a time to check in on my space and see what needs to go. Every season, my family and I declutter whatever space or spaces feel heavy. Usually, it's the kids' stuff.

THE INCOMING FLOW

Once the initial purge is finished, your focus can shift to the incoming flow of stuff. If you have humans living in your house, you're going to have a stream of stuff coming into your house on a regular basis. Kids' school papers, birthday party favors, kids' meal toys, mail, gifts from loved ones—it's just a part of life.

But remember, you are in charge. You are the one who edits your space. What comes in does not need to stay and add to the clutter pile you just got rid of. Back to one of our key mantras: what takes up your space takes up your time. You want to live in a place of balance—between letting life happen and not being overly anxious about stuff—to remain the "ruthless editor" of your home.

MAIL AND PAPERWORK

We all know how this goes. Typically, you remember to check the mail, you bring it in the house, and you set it down on the nearest surface where it sits for days or weeks (or until you have to pay that utility bill). Piles of papers are usually scattered on different surfaces in the house, avoided until you feel you have to deal with them. You realize you need a system, and it needs to be simple.

Here you go: get a magazine file box. Give it a home somewhere near your front door or whatever surface you tend to place mail and paperwork. This is going to act as an "inbox" for your physical paperwork, just like your email inbox does for you. From now on, whenever you check the mail or receive incoming papers, put them in this physical inbox.

Next, get your planner or your phone out and add a reminder to occur once a week to go through the physical inbox. My reminder is set for Sunday nights, since that's when I prep for the coming week, and I'm sort of in that zone already. You can set your reminder for Fridays or Mondays or any day you think will work best for you. And it's okay to change the day until you find your stride.

Every week, on the day of your choosing, you are going to sit down and deal with the papers in that physical inbox. Pay the bills, throw away the trash, look at the school flyers, take pictures of what you may need to reference again later and throw away the originals, and so on. I like to make this as fun as I can. I set myself up with my laptop and a cup of tea or glass of wine, turn on a TV show or some music, and just knock it out.

The thing is, almost everything can wait a week. There are very few mail or paperwork situations that are extremely urgent. If something *is* urgent, you'll know when you see it in the mail; in that case, deal with it immediately instead of adding it to the inbox.

If you love this idea of keeping a physical inbox and want more help with everything that is paper and digital clutter, I am your girl! To get yourself hooked up, visit alliecasazza .com/paperdigital.

> **TIP:** Get a folder to keep in your physical inbox and label it "in process." Sometimes things come into your home and you deal with it, but the loop isn't fully closed yet. For example, your insurance policy is about to expire, and you receive a notice in the mail. You reach out to the insurance company, but it's after business hours so it's not totally handled until you hear back from them. Place it in the in-process folder until the loop is closed.

RANDOM STUFF THE KIDS BRING HOME

Kids' meal toys, party favors, those tiny toys they get as rewards—all these things and more can be filed under "random stuff the kids bring home."

Here's how I handle them. Things like these are super cheap, which means they don't last. So, even if my kid is super psyched about the random little toy he got for doing great at the dentist, it's going to last about two seconds. I let my kids be kids and keep what they love. The last thing I want is for them to feel like they have no say or feel like the things they want to keep are in my way. That would probably send them careening into a hoarder lifestyle and that's not what I want.

And honestly, that "super special" plastic dinosaur they got at the dollar store with Aunt Sally a couple of weeks ago could end up sitting under the sofa for two weeks, forgotten, and alone. What's special now won't be special forever. Let it go and let them play. There's no need to hyper-focus on every little thing.

My kids are absolutely a part of the process, and they have a say in what stays in their space and what goes. It's kind of like a quarterly family chore that's simply a part of our lifestyle. No one really questions it, because it's a normal part of life in our home.

For now, get that planner (or your phone) back out and set a reminder. Do you feel like weekly maintenance purges would be good right now? Every other week? Monthly? Pick a schedule that feels right and write it in. This doesn't need to take a ton of time. You're just checking in, moving some things out that made their way in but aren't welcome to stay, and maintaining your role as editor of your home.

GIFTS

When someone gives you a gift, it's really about communicating emotions. Sometimes it's love, sometimes it's sympathy, other times it's gratitude. This doesn't mean you have to keep everything you are given. You can be grateful, you can acknowledge the meaning behind it, and you can remain the editor of your space. **Gifts don't come with secret contracts attached to them**, like "Here's a notepad for your desk, a matching pencil, and a card. If you get rid of this anytime before six years have passed, our friendship is over."

Obviously, nobody is thinking this way (if they do, it seems more like their issue than yours). But for whatever reason, we often feel guilty letting go of something that was given to us, even if it is absolutely not serving us.

You are on a journey. The people who love and care about you want to support you on that journey. If they understood that you'd just moved out tons of crap that had been in your way for who-knows-how-long, they would be supportive of you accepting their love but moving on from the gift. And if not, they're more focused on themselves than authentically wanting to show you love through this gift. And that, friend, is not your problem. It's not your burden to carry.

Your home; your rules. Your time cleaning up; your decisions to make about what stays. Your gift; your choice.

When I have been given something I know won't get used, isn't a good fit for me, or just needs to go, I don't declutter it out of spite or annoyance. I am truly thankful to the person who gave it (I even still write thank-you notes because my mom taught me to), and I am able to let go from a place of love and gratitude. Remember, the gift is not an obligation unless you let it be. Holding on to something given to you is doing no one any favors, especially when that gift could be donated and actually used by someone else.

If you're worried about what will happen if the gift giver asks you about the gift they gave you, it really isn't likely that such a conversation will ever take place. People tend to forget what they give you, not everyone is this rude, and it will probably be fine to tell the truth. But just in case, remember, you can say anything you need to say from a place of love and gratitude while maintaining your boundaries. It is not a crime to regift or donate. They don't even need to know you don't have the gift in your house anymore. You don't owe them anything but the gratitude you already gave.

This fear of offending is not a reason to hold on to stuff that is taking up time, energy, and space that belongs to you. It is not a good reason to keep clutter in your way. Stay focused on the whole point—less stress; more space, time, and energy; living with intention—and don't let anyone make you carry guilt that doesn't belong to you.

You are allowed to get rid of things you don't want to keep. Period.

WHAT ABOUT SHOPPING?

"Can I still shop?"

This is one question I see all the time in my community and in other minimalist spaces. If this is a question you're asking, you need to distance yourself from the "minimalist" label. Remember, labels and rules aren't helpful, so change to a different word (remember *simplicitism*?) or detach from labeling anything.

If you feel sad about any aspect of this lifestyle change, it means you're following a rule and have been invaded by legalism. You're caught in the cycle of assigning and identifying with a label that doesn't fully represent who you are and what you want.

Let me speak for myself here. I love shopping and always have. When I was growing up, my mom always took me shopping for my birthday. I would get to try on outfits and pick out a certain amount of clothes. That was my birthday gift. Even now, I love to put my headphones on, wander through the aisle of a great store, and just enjoy browsing. I'm not there to go on a shopping spree. I'm not even there to buy anything. Maybe I will, maybe I won't. For me, browsing is a fun, relaxing, enjoyable experience. I am not cutting it out of my life because of a stupid label.

For some people, though, shopping is not a nice experience but an addiction. This is a very real problem that needs to be treated as such. Know yourself and align your habits in a way that's supportive of your health and healing. If you feel you struggle with this addiction, you can find many helpful resources online. (For helpful resources about shopping addiction, visit alliecasazza.com/shoppingaddiction.)

The idea that living with less clutter or being a minimalist means you can't ever shop again is legalistic and pointless. That way of thinking can make you feel joyless and sad, which is the exact opposite of what we're trying to achieve. Remember in chapter 9 when I talked about my time with the capsule wardrobe? All I was doing was tying myself to legalistic rules, and I hated it. It was so depressing for me.

The most important step you can take when it comes to shopping is to understand the *why* behind it. When you grab your phone to open the Anthropologie app, what are you feeling? What thoughts are you having? What's going on in your life? Are you feeling neglected? Anxious? Stressed? Sad? Are you shopping because you're avoiding an issue you know you need to address? Is it your birthday and you're looking to treat yourself to a beautiful new dress? Is it simply time to replace your favorite black T-shirt that you wear so often?

Asking yourself these questions is what it means to be a *mindful shopper*. Mindful shopping doesn't mean only shopping when you really need something. It doesn't mean avoiding the store at all costs because you're afraid you're not going to be living a simple life anymore. Mindful shopping means simply being aware of why you feel the need to shop and making sure that reason is a healthy one and is serving you.

One gift you can give yourself is learning the art of appreciating without having. When I'm out at a shopping center browsing the stores, I'm in the moment. I'm enjoying myself. I love going into a store and noticing the beautiful things, getting inspired by the way they styled the mannequins, and just appreciating what I see rather than having to have it all. And sure, if I see a pair of shoes that are calling out to me, I feel free to buy them because I'm not bound by minimalism or addictive materialism. Balance. Mindfulness. Enjoyment.

Mindful shopping means having an awareness of self. It means buying things you know you'll actually use. You know exactly what you're going to wear with that sweater and which purse will match those shoes. This purchase is going to be a positive addition to your life and worthy of the space it will take up in your closet. You're not just buying something for the sake of buying it or because it was on sale. You're buying it because you need it and will use it.

Let's chat about the popular "one in, one out" rule.

The basic idea of this rule is that every time you buy something for yourself, you have to remove one thing from your closet. In theory, this is a great idea. It sets up an intentional boundary—like bumpers when you're bowling—that can help you avoid collecting endless amounts of clothing. In reality, it can feel like you're punishing yourself every time you buy something. And honestly, moms already tend to punish themselves enough. Buying a new top every now and then is something I want to encourage you to do. I feel like this rule adds an unnecessary stress.

If having a rule like this doesn't ultimately help you live how you want to live *and feel happy*, just let it go and practice mindfulness while shopping. There's no need to unnecessarily put yourself through torture just because you liked something at the store.

LET'S TALK ABOUT BIRTHDAYS AND HOLIDAYS

Picture it: you're going along, you're doing your thing, you're decluttering like a mother, and then here comes your kid's birthday (or some other celebration in which stuff is going to be coming into your home).

This is usually when panic mode hits. But I have good news, my friend. There's no need to dread the celebration seasons in your life over stuff. Dread comes from being in a place of panic and wanting to have full control. This is when I see people start to resent family and friends for buying their kids what they now see as "junk" and ruining any chance of enjoyment at birthdays and holiday parties.

Listen, no one is out to get you. It doesn't need to feel like a battle. Remember, we want you to *enjoy* your life more, not dig yourself into a panic ditch.

Let's talk about your options. You've got lots of them! Keep in mind, what I'm sharing here can work for birthdays and holidays alike.

Option 1: Do Your Normal Thing

Celebrate with a traditional party, let your kid open their gifts, smile, and be grateful. Enjoy!

I never want my kids to look back on our simple lifestyle and hate it. I'm very careful about not creating a joyless life of deprivation in the name of simplicity. Some birthdays we have parties, and my kids get gifts.

I like letting people bless my kids with gifts. It makes my kids happy, it makes the other person happy, and it makes me happy. I don't see incoming gifts from others as a threat or a burden. I see it for what it is: an expression of love. Also, it's not my job to pick up after my kids; it's theirs. I want them to learn how to manage the natural incoming flow of things and make decisions about what is worthy of staying in their space and what is not. Holidays and birthdays are an opportunity, not a hassle.

Another important thing to remember is that most people who attend birthday parties or are buying for a holiday will ask you what your child wants. It's not rude to tell them. Be honest and straightforward. This eliminates the chance that things your kids won't even use will come into your home. I've seen some moms have success by simply listing ideas on the invitations. For example, "Joey likes hot wheels, playing the Wii, and baseball." Or, "Sarah is really into Barbies and art."

Would it not be such a relief to get an invitation like that for a party your kid has been invited to? There's a chance that other parents might feel the same way, so just tell them what to get. Give them the gift of guidance.

Option 2: Celebrate Without a Traditional Party and Instead Go Somewhere for a Fun Family Experience

This is a really neat way to have a "party" without actually having a party.

Ask your kid if there's a fun place they would like to spend the day, then go! We have LEGOLAND® near where we live, and my boys love to go there on their special days. Instead of spending time and money throwing a party that they may forget about by their next birthday, spend the time and money creating an amazing experience your kid will remember forever.

You don't have to spend a ton of money. If a day at Disney World isn't in your budget, make it something simple, like a day at the zoo or a meal at their favorite restaurant. The main idea here is to let them choose something they think will be fun. It's their day!

Option 3: Celebrate with a "No Gifts" Party

Most of the time, gift giving is a happy part of a celebration that we don't want to skip. But there can be exceptions. The most important thing is how this decision is serving your family, and whether your child will still feel special on the big day.

We have hosted a "no gift" birthday party. Once when we were in the middle of a move and a miscarriage, my son, Hudson, was turning one and didn't even understand that we were having a party to celebrate him. We were in a very overwhelming, sad season and just wanted to be near friends and family, so we had a "no gifts" party. Loved ones and cake and balloons were enough to make my baby boy feel special.

Most of your family and friends just want to love on your kids, and gifts can be one way they express that. So, how do you throw a "no gifts" party without coming off as rude, annoying, or hurtful? Here are a few ideas:

- *Simply put "no gifts, please" on the invitation.* That's it. You don't have to explain yourself or say anything more. If your mother-in-law calls you, hysterical, have the conversation with her about your reasons. Set your boundaries where *you* feel they should be and stick to them!
- *Ask for an experience instead of gifts.* When people ask what your kid wants, tell them they'd really like tickets to

the zoo or the local water park. Or, if your kid is really wanting to learn a sport or an instrument, ask them to contribute to lessons. This can be a really easy and no-stress way to skip gifts but still let people feel like they're giving your kid a present.

- *Have a "fiver party."* I've seen this go well for friends in the past, and I think it's a pretty cool idea! You put on the invitation that this is a "fiver party" and then explain that all the attendee needs to bring is $5 for your kid, no gifts. They get to skip the hassle of going to the store and trying to figure out what kind of toy your kid is into, and the birthday boy or girl gets to pool together all the money and go buy something they really want. Win-win!

Remember, everything we just went over works not only for birthdays but holiday celebrations too.

Doing a purge of stuff right around a birthday or holiday is a good idea. It can help relieve stress over the incoming wave of gifts when you're on this journey to less.

You can purge before or after the big event. The perk of doing it before is that you're going to feel less overwhelmed when the birthday party or holiday comes around. The perk of doing it after is that it helps your kids make decisions. Most of the time, they're so happy about their new toys, it's easier for them to let go of older ones they aren't really using.

Whether you go to the donation center before or after the

big event or holiday, make donating about teaching your kids empathy for others rather than about just wanting a clean house. Sure, I tell my kids, "If you have less stuff, there will be less to clean up every day." But when I show them that their donations are doing good for less-fortunate people, it is deep and meaningful.

OVER-GIVERS AND BOUNDARIES

Something I see often is loved ones, who usually mean well, bringing presents over every time they visit. A lot of the women in my community struggle with this because it feels like a setback. It can even feel disrespectful or inconsiderate, especially when you've already verbalized a boundary around the incoming flow of stuff. While we can't expect everyone in our lives to get on the same page as us and jump on the simplicity bandwagon, it is your home, and you are allowed to edit what comes into it.

The first thing to remember is that most people truly just want to love on you and your kids, and gift-giving is one way they feel they are able to express their love. Acknowledge this within yourself and in your conversation with them. Most people don't know where you're coming from unless you tell them. Explain your recent journey to a life of simplicity. Explain the idea of less for the sake of more. Explain your progress and your reasons for doing this, and ask them to be a part of it with you. Ask them to help you stay on track by respecting your boundaries and lifestyle change.

Be honest about how you're feeling with the holiday coming up. If you're feeling anxious about the influx of gifts that will be coming in and are dreading the holiday for that reason, be transparent with them about it. Be vulnerable. Give them a chance to share their thoughts and feelings with you also. They may have a viewpoint you haven't considered before or their honesty may help you understand and feel gracious toward them.

If you need help expressing how you feel about receiving gifts during holidays or special occasions to others, I got you. I've written a letter you can simply copy, paste, and email to your loved ones. To get the letter, visit alliecasazza.com/letter.

———

Just remember, maintenance mode is the goal, girl. Once you get there, your life and your home are going to feel so much lighter. You'll be in the flow of living a simpler lifestyle, you'll know what to do in each area of your home as you live your life, and you can do "maintenance purges" whenever you want.

Keep in mind that if you're still feeling overwhelmed in your home, you're probably not in maintenance mode yet. You'll need to go back through your house again and declutter the specific areas we've covered in this book. You shouldn't feel overwhelmed in maintenance mode. Maintenance mode is just for maintaining the simplified home you've worked so hard to achieve. It is editing your space as you live and as things find their way into it.

AFTERWORD

You're Gonna Ruffle Some Feathers (and That's Okay!)

ALRIGHT, GIRL, IF YOU HAVEN'T ALREADY, IT'S TIME TO do the dang thing. I've given you the tools. I've walked you through the steps. I've made it as easy as possible. You're armed with tips and tricks. Let's go! It's time to take action and create this lifestyle shift.

Fair warning, though: When you start to live this way, people will notice, and not everyone will like it. Some people may even push against it or seem offended by it. When you start to live this freeing, simpler yet abundant lifestyle, you're going against the norm. You're living a counter-culture lifestyle. You're disrupting the flow. And the truth is, doing so can bring up some conviction in other people and they may project that onto you. The reason people react this way is based on their own insecurities and what they assume you think about their decisions. It really has nothing to do with you.

Even so, going against the grain and receiving pushback can be tough. That's why we have to remember *why* we're doing this in the first place. What were the thoughts, realizations, and emotions that came up in you when you decided to start being mindful of what takes up your time, space, and energy? Remember your reasons. Remember your *why* and use it as a foundation to stand on when not everyone agrees with you.

This is why minimalism is not about having less for the sake of having less. It's not about having a clean house. It's not about being a minimalist because it's trendy and cool and your house will look perfect. There has to be a bigger and deeper why. *It's about having less for the sake of having more of what matters.*

You are editing what is taking up space in your home, because you want to live a life aligned with your priorities. You no longer want to mindlessly allow things to pile up in your closet. You no longer want to look around at your over-stuffed home and think, *This is normal. Everyone lives like this. So I guess it's good enough for me.* No, you are practicing counter-cultural mindfulness for good reasons.

I've received emails from Your Uncluttered Home students who have experienced literal, life-changing results from this lifestyle shift. One woman was on the brink of an unwanted divorce. But she was able to save her marriage after implementing these changes, because she no longer created so much stress in her life, and therefore had the mental space to work on her relationship. *She created time for what mattered to her.*

Another woman shared that she felt like someone was missing from her family, but she was terrified to have another baby because of how overwhelmed she was already. After she simplified her home, she felt freer and less chronically stressed. She gave birth to a beautiful little girl whom she called "a future world changer who would not exist without this."

These stories, these changes you're making, far outweigh what others think. When you think about it this way instead of shrinking back and asking yourself, *Is this really what I want to be doing? Is this really worth it?* you start to wonder how you can apply this to everything else in your life. You begin to think of ways to create an atmosphere of less for the sake of more in your schedule, in your job, in your relationships, in your mindset, in your health and wellness.

This effort and way of life are so worthy of your energy and so helpful that you may find you're ready to simplify everywhere. Because this works. You are aware now. You know now.

Maya Angelou said: "Do the best you can until you know better. Then when you know better, do better."

You learned, you know better, and now you can do better. You are now a part of a movement of women who are choosing mindfulness and simplicity when it comes to their homes and their families. You are leaving a legacy of intention. I'm so proud of you!

Make sure you don't stay on the outskirts! I want you on the inside, as part of the group that is supporting, encouraging, and cheering on other women in their journeys—just like they'll be doing for you. We're all in this together; we need one another.

There's a whole world online that I've created to support you.

THE PURPOSE SHOW PODCAST

My podcast is a vault of life inspiration for you, mama! With millions of downloads and loads of episodes to choose from (and more uploaded each week), you are all set with audio support as you shift the way you do motherhood.

Go to alliecasazza.com/podcast.

THE FACEBOOK GROUP

If you want to ask questions, share before and after photos for accountability, or make friends who are on the same journey as you, join our community. You are welcome here.

Go to alliecasazza.com/community.

INSTAGRAM

This is an encouraging space where you can not only see this lifestyle in action but connect on a deeper level with me as I personally share my life with you each day. You'll find quotes, action steps, pep talks, and live streams that will keep you moving forward.

Follow me @allie_thatsme.

PROGRAMS

A real, deep change happens at this next level. My programs are world-renowned and designed to quite literally change your life. If you want that, it's all here for you. You're the hero in your story, mama. I'm just here to clear the path and guide you through the changes you need to make so your story is one you're proud of.

To browse these programs, go to alliecasazza.com/programs. For your exclusive discount on the Your Uncluttered Home course, go to alliecasazza.com/course.

———

You are so amazing, you're such a good mom, and you're so supported. I see you, girl. You've so got this.

Rooting for you always,

xo Allie

ACKNOWLEDGMENTS

No one accomplishes anything alone.

—LESLIE KNOPE

I CAN'T ACKNOWLEDGE THE PEOPLE WHO HAVE COME alongside me in writing this without first acknowledging my God, my Source of all good, my Creator, and my Guide. You are the God who sees me, pulls me upward, sits with me quietly, dances with me in the living room, and roots me in Love. Thank you for showing me the way out of the pit. Thank you for these words. Thank you for the moments on our walks where you breathed life into me when I was tired. I love you.

To my sweetest friend, Brian. It's too much to list in a space as small as this—but thank you. Thank you for being a safe, sturdy, emotional container for me through this process. Thank you for the time you sat quietly while I melted down in the car in Greenville over this project. Thank you for the times you said, "Just go get in the shower and clarity will come." Even though that kind of pissed me off, it was true every time, and I needed it. Thank you for taking endless amounts of walks with me so I could "talk it out." Thank you for all the times you made me a breakfast shake (seeds?) and came into my office bearing coffee and nourishing food. Thank you for getting me a book-shaped cake when I got my deal—my dream deal! Thank you for all of it. Everything. I'm glad I married you and, like, had lots of babies and stuff with you. ;)

To Bella, my girl. Thanks for watching me climb and seeing the journey for what it was. Thanks for being in it with me. Thanks for caring about the details. I love you. Girls rule.

To my boys, Leland, Hudson, and Emmett. Thank you for all the clapping, cheering, and celebrating along the way, my loves! And thank you for playing Donkey Kong 2 with me during my writing breaks. You may never know how much that helped me get this done.

Hayley, my beloved little Gemini. I adore you, seriously. Has there ever been a more perfect pair than the two of us? We are #babessupportbabes personified. Thank you for that support—all of it. You didn't hold back in giving that to me, and I cannot even begin to tell you how grateful I am. Thank you for sitting with me in that Zoom room, time and time again. Thank you for being a sounding board, giving advice, typing for me, laughing with me, being *in* it with me. Thank you for taking things off my plate. Thank you for giving me permission. Thank you for getting amped up and cursing like a sailor during the photo shoot. Thank you for sharing your energy with me when I had none. Thank you for standing next to me and holding my hand through it all. Bitches be slayin'. I love you.

To Amy. You are everything that I am not but is still necessary and expected of me to be in the role I'm in. I don't think you realize how grateful I am for you. The way you are, exactly as you are without any performing or earning, is perfect. You are so extremely special to me. Thank you for reading and rereading this book. Thank you for being detail oriented when I literally cannot be. Thank you for holding space for my emotions and self-doubt. Thank you for sharing all of this with me. Thank you for being absolutely brilliant. You change lives every single day, doing what you do in this company. I see you, I love you, and I will be by your side in anything you go through as long as you let me, because you have done that for me. *Thank you.*

To Jenni Burke, my beautiful, strong, intelligent literary agent. You helped make my dream happen, and it was wilder than my wildest version of it. So what you really did was teach me to dream bigger and aim higher. And for that, I can never thank you enough. Your constant support, your encouraging emails and voxes, your smiling face, and your friendship mean so much to me. Thank you, Jenni.

To Anna. Thank you for sitting with me in Zoom week after week at the beginning of this project. You were my fingers when I needed to talk this book into existence before actually sitting in front of the keyboard myself. That was *so* helpful for me! Thank you. I will not forget all the times I made your pregnant belly contract from laughing at my far-too-inappropriate-for-the-book jokes and you had to get up to pee. Love you, girl. Thank you.

To Jenny Baumgartner, my editor. You have been a teacher, and I am beyond grateful to you. Thank you for believing in my message as hard as you do. Thank you for making me a better communicator through this process.

To DJ, of Pretzel Day. Thank you for believing in my vision, both for this book and the cover. Thank you for staying up all night, multiple nights in a row, to get the design done at the last minute when it was all down to the wire and the pressure was weighing down on me. You came in and carried that with me, and I felt less alone. Your talent is incredible, but it can't touch the human being you are. Thank you.

To my OG family. Thank you for being excited for me, for supporting me, going out to dinner with me, and calling me to check in. Thanks for the group texts and for sending stupid videos to provide a much-needed distraction during the tough parts of this process.

Mom, thank you for teaching me everything you have! Thank you for showing me how to get through hard things and how to be a mom and also a person. Thanks for encouraging my writing when I was a kid. It was an outlet, a way to express, and an art for me, and you always seemed to see that and encouraged it. Thank you for buying me countless books that opened up my mind and showed me a world where people get paid to spread a message, igniting a deep desire in me to do the same. And here we are. ;)

Dad, thank you for taking me on those drives to Anaheim

when I was a kid. You could've left me home and gotten a break, but you didn't, and I owe my character and strength to that. You introduced me to really good music and talked to me about what it means to be strong, to be a leader, to stand for what's right, to be a voice. You taught me to take no shit, and look how much I ended up needing that! I love you.

To Jules, my soul sister and friend of twenty-seven years. How cool is it that after all this time, all our dreaming, all our memories made and life lived side by side, it was you that I was with when the offers started pouring in? I left for our girls' trip feeling vulnerable, out on a ledge, and terrified that no one would see the value in what I'd built. Being in Nashville, with my sister friend, reading those proposed deals and realizing that that was *it* . . . it was an experience I won't ever forget. And there's no one else I'd rather have experienced that with. Thank you for doing childhood with me, and continuing to do life with me, even if that looks different than we thought it would when we were girls. I love you.

To Daniel, thank you for the random and incredibly supportive voxes, and for all the research and fact checking you did for me and this book. Thank you for your diligent search for that one damn study that apparently came from nowhere. Your friendship and how hilarious you are is woven within the foundation of this book. Thank you, friend.

To my friend Tanya Dalton, thank you for being in my corner. Thanks for the advice, the laughs, the venting sessions, the Zoom calls, the Voxer marathons, and the friendship. Cheers to our books, girl.

To my old and new friend, Lauren. Thanks for being the

gentle observer of this book cover process, for being flexible AF, and for sending love and light every step of the way. Lauren Pollard Photography was a part of this book, its cover, and this entire process. Thank you for pumping me up, for dancing to Lizzo with me, and for shooting me twice. Thank you for encouraging me and seeing me through this. Love and light, but also . . . ;)

This book, along with my message, came from a struggle I don't ever want to relive. A struggle I want to help other women avoid altogether or come out from quickly if they're already in it. So, to the women in my online community and those who have shared their stories with me, shared my message, tagged me on Instagram—I see you, I love you, and I'm with you and for you.

And finally, to everyone who preferred me when I was still playing small, thank you for your words, thank you for the lessons you gave me, thank you for everything. But I especially want to thank you for giving me fuel to keep going.

APPENDIX

Stories from Women in My

Online Community

KANDIS BABEL (@KANDISBABEL)

Mom of four in Cincinnati, OH; student of
Simplify Your Homeschool®, Your Happiest
Holidays®, and The Supermom Vault®

MY LIFE WAS CHAOTIC AT BEST. AFTER CHOOSING TO
quit teaching in a public school setting to be a stay-at-home
mom, I was restless and felt like I lacked purpose. Staying
home with my kids was something that I'd always known I
wanted to do, but things weren't functioning.

A year into my stay-at-home life, I started working in
ministry about ten hours a week. During that time, we added
another baby to our family. I was staying up until two or
three in the morning writing curriculum for children's ministry and looking for volunteers while also taking care of my
kids and trying to take care of our house.

Our home became a disaster zone; my stress and anxiety went through the roof. I decided my home was a disaster zone because we lived in too small a house on the wrong side of town, so we moved. But we moved all our stuff with us. The longer I lived there, the more I realized that this move hadn't made anything easier. I was so frustrated, because I felt like I couldn't find an end to this crazy cycle.

About a year after our move, a friend of mine introduced me to Allie's podcast, *The Purpose Show*. This friend had been decluttering, and I thought her life seemed so much easier than mine. I listened to all the podcast episodes but did very little with what I learned.

I just kept spinning my wheels, totally frustrated. A few months later, I was ready to quit the ministry because it seemed like the easiest way to redeem some time. I prayed and cried and prayed some more, but when I opened my email to resign from my ministry position, there was an email from Allie. I opened it and a light bulb came on! She said my work wasn't my problem; my stuff, my mindset, and my lack of routines were my problem.

After that, I followed Allie's advice and started going through the house slowly. I went through my whole kitchen and cut it by at least half. I went through all our clothes and cut the amount we had back, and our laundry suddenly got lighter.

During this time, our third baby was born with medical issues; yet, even with more thrown into the mix, I realized I was no longer staying up until two or three in the morning working.

The most surprising side effect for me has been the joy I now have in my motherhood. I liked being a mom before, but now it's fun. And my kids have been positively affected by this new lifestyle as well. My oldest is so much more creative now because he has space to be. My kids play outside, and they all play together now. Having less stuff allowed them to bond better.

Greater than any of that—and let's face it, all of that in and of itself is pretty great—I'm following my calling. I'm still working in children's ministry, and I've increased to working full-time happily because I have the margin in my life to do so.

WHITNEY DOYLE (@THIS_IS_WHITNEYCAROL)

Mom of two in Bellingham, WA; student of Your Uncluttered Home® and Unburdened®

The year I got engaged, my mom and stepdad divorced. They didn't divide their things, so my new husband and I accepted most of the belongings they had accumulated for more than a decade. This meant we had to find a bigger (and more expensive) apartment, which added stress and affected my decision to either work full-time or go to school. I basically had to arrange my goals and dreams to accommodate stuff. Eventually, we bought a house and filled it, plus the large two-car garage and a storage unit, with all our things.

I stopped trying to get ahead [of stuff cluttering my

house] and just started stashing everything in order to make the home function. I had no clarity on what should stay, so I kept almost everything, which was way too much. For years, I avoided weekend plans to organize and reorganize. I even opted to "celebrate" my birthday by working on the mountain of stuff in the garage while my kids played in the yard without me. My kids started saying things like, "Oh, you know how Mom is. She likes to organize." I was too busy, distracted, and emotionally preoccupied. I have way more memories of dealing with toys than actually playing with them with my kids.

I felt like I was obviously not good at this motherhood thing. I felt I wasn't good at being domestic or at connecting with my kids. I thought I was a failure and that I was never going to measure up. I had a healthy family and lived the traditional (supposed) dream life, but I never had the energy or time to participate in it, much less enjoy it. The moments when I did choose to be present always came at the expensive cost of neglecting myself or the chores I could never keep up with. I just thought it was normal to feel exhausted and burned out.

I increased pressure on my husband to step up and fill in the gaps. That extended from the physical tasks of running a home to being the main emotionally available parent for the kids. I ugly cried on my bathroom floor the night before my oldest child's fifth birthday, grieving because his formative years were over, and I felt like I'd failed him. It still makes me cry to even think about that. I'll never forget the day I finally just gave up. I turned to a mom friend for real hope, but only found empathy and solidarity. She told me, "Maybe the idea of this being the most magical time just isn't accurate. It's just really hard!" I grieved that I had no more fight in me to prove her wrong.

I withdrew from any interests and relationships. I hoped no one would ask how things were going or why I hadn't pursued a former project I once gushed about. I thought I was just not good enough. The scary rage I struggled with, the missed time with my babies, my failed business ventures, and neglected hobbies became a culmination of stress that led to one moment. While house shopping online, I was flipping through pictures and the view of one backyard stopped me. It was on a cliff so you could see for forever. I stopped and said to my husband, "Do you ever just want to fall off a cliff like that? Not to splat or anything. Just to fall, so you would actually physically feel all the powerlessness?"

That was the moment we knew everything *must* change. We ordered a giant dumpster and filled it *three* times. Everything got so much better, but I still avoided commitments and made sure everyone in the home knew how important it was to stay on top of everything.

One day, I found Allie's resources and realized that I had only scratched the surface. She gave me the plan I needed to follow through. She explained how to make your own rules. The other minimalist extremes out there were just unrealistic for me. It was all so black and white. Allie's version of minimalism allowed me to cater it to mom-life, and she told me how to do that step-by-step instead of me just doing it in a trial-and-error kind of way.

I dove completely in, and within five months I created a

purposeful home. My storage unit was emptied for good, and the biggest thing of all happened: I found hope and purpose.

I remembered who I was as a person. I had dreams and goals. I was an intentional person with a fierce passion and an impact to make. I'm able to be sincerely present with my kids and enjoy them consistently. I play with my kids now because it naturally flows out of me; I have energy for it. All this while I'm growing my wellness brand (shout out to Allie's business training too!), starting a podcast, improving our homeschool experience, and even adding a few extra side hustles!

Getting rid of my clutter gave me freedom, purpose, and momentum. Grateful just doesn't even cut it.

If I could say one thing to anyone reading this book who thinks they have things under control and they can do it without help, I would challenge them to look at the sustainability of what they're maintaining. I thought I was a minimalist when I purged three dumpsters full of things, but I still couldn't maintain that lifestyle well. I maintained it through my own grit, not from systems. Allie gave me a system that maintains itself.

MARISA MONACHINO (@MARISA_MONACHINO)

Mom of four in Rochester, NY; student of Your
Uncluttered Home® and Uncluttered Kids®

I used to be a clean, organized person. My floors were vacuumed and mopped daily by 10 a.m.—and this was with two kids! But after baby number three, my whole life started to change. I couldn't tackle the laundry, I couldn't clean my floors, I couldn't get my kitchen presentable. Everything in my house was a disaster. The way I was living was so different from who I knew I was. By the time I had my fourth baby, I had accepted that this was my life now, and it felt so hard.

I first discovered Allie from a friend's Facebook post and joined in on the Declutter Like a Mother challenge. I was immediately hooked. I spent the last $200 in our savings account to purchase Allie's Your Uncluttered Home course, and it was a game changer for me. I realized just how much holding on to the excess stuff was holding me back. My life wasn't the problem; my stuff was.

Allie's version of minimalism has helped me get rid of the all-or-nothing, perfectionist mindset that I tend to have. I didn't have a lot of time when I started all of this, so I fit in decluttering in the spare fifteen- or thirty-minute spurts I would find in my day. I had four kids, nine and under, when I started on this journey. That is a full-time thing. I was getting other people's kids off the bus to make a little extra money. I was going to school four hours a night, four nights a week, working at a salon every other weekend, and also had a side gig on the weekends. I was so busy, but I found the time to declutter because it was worth it to me. I made it happen. I had to. And it's almost like a muscle. The more you work it, the easier it becomes.

Every facet of my life has changed. I've been able to start constructing my life in a meaningful way. Decluttering opened up more intentionality in my life and how I wanted to live my life. I've been able to pursue the career I wanted. I've been able to give more to my family. I connect with my kids every day. I've made space to pursue my faith. I've started meditation. I've pursued my dream of working at a law firm.

This is so much more than just minimizing your stuff. It's an entirely life-changing journey.

Now I wake up and feel like I can tackle my day. And my family has been positively affected too. My husband and kids can enjoy more of me, and they're on board with this lifestyle. Taking control of my own stuff has made a huge difference.

Minimalism started me down a path of self-improvement. Prior to following Allie, I never thought to ask myself if the things I was doing were aligned with my purpose. Now that I do, I have control over so much of how my life looks. This has saved my motherhood and made my life so fulfilled.

I want to tell other women to just give it a try. You have nothing to lose by trying. And everything to gain.

DIJON RUSSELL (@DIJON_RUSSELL)

Mom of five in Lubbock, TX; student of Your
Uncluttered Home® and Unburdened®

A few years ago, I was married with a five-year-old and a baby girl. Life was hectic but good. I navigated through it by holding on to everything "just in case." Clutter was my normal. Stress was my normal. Crazy was my normal.

A couple of years later, we began to foster an amazing fifteen-year-old girl and her one-year-old son. Soon after, our biological son was born, and we brought home our eleven-year-old foster daughter. In a matter of six months, we went from having two kids in our home to six kids.

My house was always messy and the laundry never ended. I hated my home, and I was becoming a person I didn't recognize anymore. I wanted to be a fun mom, but there was no room for that in my life. There was only room for maintaining, cleaning, folding, and washing stuff. My cousin told me to check out Allie Casazza.

I found *The Purpose Show* that day, and so many light bulbs started going off for me. When I heard Allie say that you don't just buy stuff with your money but also with your time, everything started expanding for me. I dove in. This was just what my family needed. I binged on all her podcast episodes in a week and shortly after purchased her Your Uncluttered Home course and took action.

We decluttered toys, laundry, dishes, and set an intention for each room. My whole family started loving these new changes!

Allie's way of simplifying gave me the ability to do what was right for me and our family. Being able to come at minimalism with more open guidelines and being able to feel into what is good and right for my children is huge, because sometimes my kids, especially the ones who come out of the foster system, are attached to their things, and it would be damaging to them for me to go in and say they can't keep something because of some stupid rule. So being able to feel into that and do what is right for our family is freeing.

Gaining this kind of freedom at home sparked a new hope inside me. I began saying no to draining obligations and yes to creating again. The white space and margin that I needed was found in the absence of all the stuff. The mother and the woman I wanted to be was found there too. My life felt very black and white before. It felt very methodical. It felt almost empty. It felt frustrating. Simplifying my life gave it color, purpose, and margin.

Now I have more brain space for my job. I have dreams for starting my own business. I have goals for buying my daughter her own home. I have a side hustle in children's entertainment, and I employ a couple of people. I've gone on mission trips while my husband has stayed home with the kids, and my husband has gone on mission trips while I stay home with the kids, and it's not stressful. Our house doesn't fall apart, because we have less stuff and systems in place. We go on regular date nights, and it kind of put the fun back into our marriage because, honestly, we don't fight about stuff anymore.

What if life really isn't supposed to be like this? What if motherhood really is supposed to be joyful? What if it is supposed to be fulfilling? What if you don't ever move from this place of overwhelm? What gifts are you leaving on the table and never realizing?

Taking this step is probably the most important step anyone will ever take, because it will allow you to realize who is inside of you.

NOTES

1. Jack Feuer, "The Clutter Culture," *UCLA Magazine*, July 1, 2012, http://magazine.ucla.edu/features/the-clutter-culture/.
2. Allie Casazza, "How Getting Rid of My Stuff Saved My Motherhood," The Balanced Life, August 22, 2016, https://thebalancedlifeonline.com/how-getting-rid-of-my-stuff-saved-my-motherhood/.
3. Marshall Goldsmith and Mark Reiter, *Triggers: Creating Behavior That Lasts—Becoming the Person You Want to Be* (New York: Crown Business, 2015), 38.
4. John Tierney, "Do You Suffer from Decision Fatigue?" *New York Times Magazine*, August 17, 2011, https://www.nytimes.com/2011/08/21/magazine/do-you-suffer-from-decision-fatigue.html.
5. Lisa Kogan, "Nate Berkus: Why You Should Break the Rules When Decorating Your Home," Oprah.com, February 8, 2011, http://www.oprah.com/home/nate-berkus-home-decorating-advice-home-design/all.
6. Letter to the author on September 29, 2020, from Sami Womack, student of Your Uncluttered Home and Unburdened. Used with permission. Follow her on Instagram @asunnysideuplife.
7. Catherine A. Roster, Joseph R. Ferrari, and Martin Peter Jurkat, "The Dark Side of Home: Assessing Possession 'Clutter' on Subjective Well-Being," *Journal of Environmental Psychology* 46 (March 2016): 32–41, https://www.researchgate.net/publication/298428874_The_dark_side_of_home_Assessing_possession_'clutter'_on_subjective_well-being.

8. Jack Feuer, "The Clutter Culture."

9. Annie Dillard, *The Writing Life* (New York: Harper Perennial, 1998).

10. Elke Schubert and Rainer Strick, *Toy-Free Kindergarten: A Project to Prevent Addiction for Children and with Children* (Munich, Germany: Aktion Jugendschutz, 1996), http://www .spielzeugfreierkindergarten.de/pdf/englisch.pdf; and Carly Dauch, Michelle Imwalle, Brooke Ocasio, and Alexia E. Metz, "The Influence of the Number of Toys in the Environment on Toddlers' Play," *Infant Behavior and Development* 50 (February 2018): 78–87, https://www.sciencedirect.com/science/article /abs/pii/S0163638317301613?via%3Dihub.

11. Ray A. Smith, "A Closet Filled with Regrets," *Wall Street Journal*, April 17, 2013, https://www.wsj.com/articles/SB1000142412788 7324240804578415002232186418.

ABOUT THE AUTHOR

ALLIE CASAZZA IS ON A MISSION TO ERADICATE THE "Hot Mess Mom" stereotype by empowering other women. She has built a massive platform, reaching hundreds of thousands of women with her proven, family-oriented approach to minimalism. She is also the host of *The Purpose Show*, a chart-topping podcast, and the creator of multiple online courses that have generated millions of dollars. Her platform continues to grow every day as more women discover her life-changing approach to creating an abundant life. She lives in Greenville, South Carolina, with her husband, Brian, where they homeschool their four young children.